The
ROTHBURY BRANCH

by
Stanley C. Jenkins, M.A.

THE OAKWOOD PRESS

© Oakwood Press and S.C. Jenkins 1991

ISBN 0 85361 420 2

Typeset by Gem Publishing Company, Brightwell, Wallingford, Oxfordshire.

Printed by Alpha Print Ltd, Witney.

Oakwood Press books by the same author

The *Oxford, Worcester & Wolverhampton Railway* (joint author)
The *Great Western & Great Central Joint Railway*
The *Fairford Branch*
The *Lynn & Hunstanton Railway*
The *Wells-next-the-Sea Branch*
The *Cromer Branch*
The *Moretonhampstead & South Devon Railway* (joint author)
The *Watford to St Albans Branch*
The *Northampton & Banbury Junction Railway*
The *Alston Branch*
The *Leek and Manifold Light Railway*

Acknowledgements

Thanks are due to the staffs of the University of Leicester library, the Public Record Office, and other record repositories, for assistance during the early stages of research. Also to Ian Futers, who generously provided me with a file of NCR and Wansbeck Railway material, together with a useful assortment of photographs. Other help came from Lens of Sutton, R.M. Casserley, Barry Nicholson, J.W. Armstrong, E.E. Smith, A.J. Wickens, F.W. Hampson, J. Addyman, W.S. Sellar and J. Scott.

A Note on Proper Nouns

Name changes can be a cause of great confusion, and it is therefore worth pointing out that the NER station at Coldstream was originally called 'Cornhill' – the latter name being used in the Northumberland Central Act (and other contemporary documents). Scotsgap was sometimes spelled Scots Gap or Scot's Gap, while NCR promoter Sir John Swinburne was occasionally referred to as Sir John Swinburn.

Published by
The OAKWOOD PRESS
P.O.Box 122, Headington, Oxford.

Contents

Introduction

The North British Railway was one of the larger pre-1923 companies, but
its position in the northern part of the British Isles means that it has received
relatively little attention from railway enthusiasts or photographers.
Although not an exclusively Scottish company, the NBR was firmly based in
the Edinburgh region and in the Kingdom of Fife, and in 1923 the company
contributed over 1,300 route miles to the newly-formed London & North
Eastern Railway (a mileage second only to that of the NER in the LNER
group).

For branch line enthusiasts, the NBR system provides a large selection of attractive single line routes; one thinks, for example, of the Aberfoyle and Langholm branches, or of the equally-picturesque Leadburn to Dolphinton route. Few of these lines were ever traversed by southern-based enthusiasts, and it is no exaggeration to say that, as far as most English travellers are concerned, the branch lines of the North British Railway were *terra incognita*. Perhaps surprisingly, a significant proportion of the NBR's secondary mileage was on the English side of the border, and insofar as these lines were 'Scottish Railways in England' they are of particular interest to the enthusiast. The lines concerned included long cross country routes such as the Border Counties and Wansbeck Valley routes, and shorter dead-end lines such as the Silloth, Port Carlisle, and Rothbury branches. This present study is based on the Rothbury line but, as Rothbury trains ran through to Morpeth over the Wansbeck Railway, the narrative will also contain fleeting references to the latter route.

The story of the Rothbury branch is, in many ways, a familiar one. Built by a group of private landowners, it was not a commercial success, and the line's original owners soon sold their poverty-stricken undertaking to a neighbouring main line company (in this case the North British Railway). Thereafter, the branch served the local community in a useful, but unspecta-cular way, for three-quarters-of-a-century, though lack of potential traffic meant that its passenger services were withdrawn as long ago as 1952. Goods services survived for another 11 years until, in 1963, the Rothbury to Scotsgap Junction line was closed in its entirety.

The story of the Rothbury branch falls naturally into five chapters; Chapter One deals with the promotion of the line while the following chapter describes the construction, opening and early years of the railway. Chapters Three and Five deal with the subsequent history of the line, and Chapter Four describes the route and stations in detail. It is hoped that the resulting monograph will be of interest to both railway enthusiasts and local historians, and serve as a fitting memorial to an interesting rural line that is no more.

A picturesque view of Rothbury and the River Coquet captured on an early postcard published by Graham of Morpeth.   *Oakwood Collection*

Historical Summary

Companies of Origin

Wansbeck Railway: Formed 8th August, 1859 to build a railway between Morpeth and Reedsmouth Junction, on the Border Counties line; amalgamated with the North British Railway in July 1863.

Northumberland Central Railway: Incorporated 28th July, 1863 with Powers to build a line from the Wansbeck Railway, near Hartburn to Ford, with a branch to Cornhill on the Berwick and Kelso section of the North Eastern Railway. Capital Powers of £270,000 in £10 shares and borrowing Powers for a further £90,000; amalgamated with the North British Railway in July 1872.

Dates of Opening

Morpeth to Scotgap (Wansbeck Railway) opened 23rd July, 1862.
Scotsgap to Rothbury (Northumberland Central) opened 1st November, 1870.

Dates of Closure

Morpeth to Rothbury closed to passengers on Saturday 13th September, 1952, remaining open for freight traffic until November 1963, when the Scotsgap to Rothbury line was closed to all traffic. The remaining section from Morpeth to Scotsgap and thence to Woodburn was closed to all traffic in 1966.

Distances

Morpeth–Scotsgap Junction	11 miles	11 chains
Scotsgap Junction–Rothbury	13 miles	4 chains
Morpeth–Rothbury	24 miles	15 chains

Acts of Parliament

Wansbeck Railway 8th August, 1859: incorporation.
Northumberland Central Railway 28th July, 1863 (26 & 27 Vic. cap. 324): incorporation.
Northumberland Central Railway 12th April, 1867 (30 Vic. cap. 9): reduction of capital and abandonment of route beyond Rothbury.

Typical Motive Power

North British 'R' class 4–4–0Ts and 'C' class 0–6–0s worked on the line for many years, but former North Eastern Railway 'G5' 0–4–4Ts and 'J21' 0–6–0s were used from the 1920s onwards.

Mode of Operation

Single line between Scotsgap Junction and Rothbury with crossing loops at Rothbury and Scotsgap, and a refuge siding at Ewesley. Initially worked by One-Engine-in Steam, later by Electric Tablet.

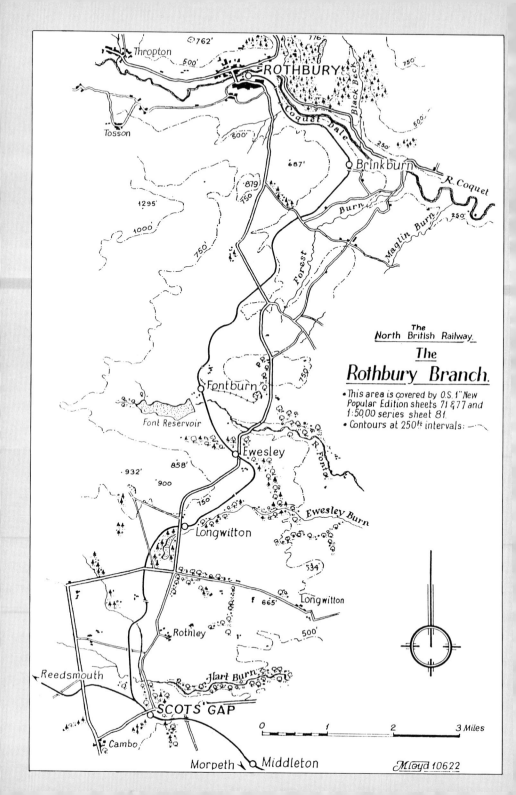

Chapter One
Origins of the Line (1855–1863)

Situated in England's northernmost county, the little Northumberland town of Rothbury occupies a picturesque position in a bend of the River Coquet. Once known as 'Routhbyrig', the town was, in former times, a frontier settlement in the disputed borderlands between England and Scotland. Feuding, murder and robbery were, in consequence, a way of life, and on occasions these endless border conflicts culminated in full-scale warfare. In 1311, for example, a Scottish army invaded the northern marches, laying waste Coquetdale and neighbouring Redesdale before retiring northwards.

In Tudor times, England and Scotland moved closer together in the face of foreign aggression, but the inhabitants of the borderlands retained their reputation for lawlessness, and when Bernard Gilpin ('The Apostle of the North') attempted to preach in Rothbury he found the church full of armed men. A full-scale riot was clearly in the offing, but when 'their weapons made a clashing sound and the one side drew nearer to the other so that they were in danger to fall to blows in the midst of the church' he descended from the pulpit to prevent an affray!

Rothbury was not, in pre-Victorian times, a particularly wealthy place, its economy being based mainly upon the needs of an upland agricultural area – although there was a tract of somewhat richer land to the north. The town also benefited from its geographical location as a minor route centre in the Scottish borderlands, and travellers en route to Scotland, Newcastle, or elsewhere no doubt brought at least some custom to local traders and inn keepers. To outsiders, mid-18th century Rothbury appeared to be a mean, shabby-looking place, and a contemporary writer was clearly unimpressed by his visit to the historic border town:

> Rothbury is a poor town of two streets which are not paved, and the houses are mostly thatched; they cover them with sods for warmth, and thatch with heath, which will last thirty years. There are turnpike roads from it to Hexham, Newcastle, Morpeth and Alnwick, which make it a thoroughfare from all the villages to the west and north and Ellesden, for there is no other town this way to the west or north; the rise of the Coquet, which is pronounced Cocket, being the bounds of Scotland at about twelve miles distant.
>
> It is a market town and they have some fairs chiefly for black cattle; and wool is sent from this place to Newcastle. They have several shops and handicrafts exercised here, particularly that of hatters . . . I went half a mile down the river to see the Thrum where the river falls about 40 yards through a narrow passage between the rocks about five feet wide. The salmon comes here in November to spawn, but they are not permitted to fish them.

In an age of closely-spaced, thatched houses, fire was an ever-present hazard, and complete devastation was by no means uncommon. It is well-known that London burned down in 1666, but such calamities also struck in smaller communities, and Rothbury was burned down on no less than three occasions! The first of these great fires occured in 1738, and there were subsequent conflagrations in 1782 and 1785. One beneficial aspect of major fires is that they often lead to improved town planning, and something of this nature evidently took place in Rothbury which, by the early 19th century, had been transformed into a largely stone-built town, with several simple, but attractive, Georgian buildings.

In later years, Rothbury settled down to become a typical country town, and by mid-Victorian times the town had become the marketing centre for the surrounding area. The parish church was entirely rebuilt in 1849–50, and at a time of increasing national prosperity, many new buildings were erected during the next few years. Rothbury would clearly have benefited from the provision of rail transport facilities, but there were, at first glance, few incentives for large main line railway companies to serve Rothbury directly.

Early Railway Development

Railways arrived in the Scottish borders at a surprisingly early date, one of the first lines to appear being the pioneering Brampton Railway, which had been opened (with horse traction) as far back as 1798. Although primarily a mineral line, the Brampton Railway, which ran from Brampton to collieries in the Hallbankgate area on the Cumberland–Northumberland border, introduced steam locomotives in the 1830s, and in 1837 Stephenson's famous *Rocket* was acquired for further use on this historic line. Further east, the Stockton & Darlington Railway was another early steam-worked line, while the north eastern industrial areas are justly regarded as the birthplace of the World's railways.

The success of the Liverpool & Manchester Railway in the 1830s demonstrated that rail transport was a viable proposition, and in the 1840s companies such as the Lancaster & Carlisle Railway (incorporated 6th June, 1844) and the Caledonian Railway (formed 31st July, 1845) were promoted to forge vital north-south links between England and Scotland. When opened, these new lines became (with their allies further south) part of the West Coast main line, while over on the east coast the North British, North Eastern and Great Northern companies eventually formed a rival north-south trunk route between England and Scotland. In the meantime, the Newcastle & Carlisle Railway had been formed to build a cross country link between the West Coast main line at Carlisle and the East Coast route at Newcastle.

Although generally regarded as a purely Scottish company, the North British Railway was willing to support lines on the English side of the border, and in this context, Richard Hodgson (1812–1877) the NBR Chairman, was destined to play a central role. A Northumberland resident who sat in Parliament as the representative of an English constituency, he was able to portray himself as the Chairman of a truly national, Anglo-Scottish company, and under his forceful leadership the North British Railway successfully promoted the Border Union line between Edinburgh and Carlisle. Designed to furnish the NBR with a main line to England which would be entirely independent of the rival Caledonian system, the Border Union Railway (Waverley route) was opened to passenger traffic on 1st July, 1862.

Meanwhile, a local company known as the Border Counties Junction Railway had been incorporated to build a branch from the Newcastle &

Carlisle Railway at Hexham to a place known as Belling Burn near Plashetts; the Border Counties Junction was built in 1855–56, and in 1857 a further Act was obtained for an extension from Plashetts to Riccarton Junction, on the Border Union line. This section of line was opened (simultaneously with the Border Union route) on 1st July, 1862, and the ambitious North British Railway thereby gained two useful cross-border lines from which to launch further attacks deep into English territory.

The Border Union and Border Counties lines were clearly part of one grand design which, if successfully completed, would have given the NBR direct access to both Carlisle and Newcastle. Richard Hodgson and his fellow-North British Directors hoped to consolidate their scheme by gaining control of the Newcastle & Carlisle Railway, but in the event the N & CR was absorbed by the rival North Eastern Railway, and the NBR Directors had to be content with running powers over the N & CR line between Hexham and Newcastle.

Having failed to grasp control of the Newcastle & Carlisle Railway, the NBR could still hope to reach Newcastle via the Wansbeck Railway, which had been authorised by an Act of Parliament dated 8th August, 1859. The Wansbeck promoters hoped to build at 25¼ mile cross country line from the Blyth & Tyne Railway at Morpeth to Reedsmouth Junction – at which point connection would be made with the Border Counties line. With full North British backing, the Wansbeck Railway was opened in stages, the first section, from Morpeth to Scotsgap, being completed on 23rd July, 1862, while the portion from Scotsgap to Knowesgate was opened to traffic in June 1864. Finally, on 1st May, 1865, the Wansbeck Valley Railway was opened throughout to its junction with the Border Counties line at Reedsmouth Junction.

The Wansbeck Railway was initially worked by the Blyth & Tyne Railway, but the completion of the link to Reedsmouth Junction enabled the hitherto-isolated Wansbeck line to be physically connected to the parent NBR company, and thereafter the line was worked by North British locomotives and rolling stock; indeed, the Wansbeck Railway had already been absorbed by the NBR, full amalgamation having taken place in July 1863.

The Border Union, Border Counties and Wansbeck railways constituted a sizeable system, but the inhabitants of small towns and villages such as Rothbury, Wooler and Milfield were not satsified with these new facilities, and there were, in the early 1860s, demands for still more railways in the remote, central Northumberland region.

Formation of the Northumberland Central Railway Co.

Encouraged by the successful promotion of the neighbouring Border Union, Border Counties and Wansbeck Valley railways, the landowners of Rothbury, Wooler and the surrounding area were especially keen to see the benefits of rail transport brought to their own farms and estates. Richard Hodgson, the Chairman of the North British Railway (and himself an important local landowner) was active behind the scenes throughout this formative period, and under his guidance several public and private meetings were held in an attempt to stimulate support for a railway linking Cold-stream, Crookham, Akeld, Wooler, Wooperton, Rothbury and the Wans-beck Valley line at Scotsgap. One of the most important of these meetings took place at Morpeth on 25th October, 1862; the meeting was attended by several prominent landowners, all of whom supported the proposed railway and hoped to see the route in operation in the near future. Having unani-mously agreed that the scheme was worthy of support, the promoters formed a provisional committee to collect subscriptions and prepare a Bill for presentation to Parliament in the coming session.

It was hoped that the Bill could be lodged without undue expenditure, £2,000 being suggested as the likely cost of the scheme up to the deposit of the Bill. To keep preliminary costs within reasonable bounds the solicitor and Engineer agreed to confine their charges to 'out of pocket' expenses until the Bill was passed; the railway itself would be known as 'The Northumber-land Central' line – an appropriate appellation for this important cross-country route through the very centre of Northumberland.

The Northumberland Central Railway was, from its very inception, a landowners' company, and its leading supporters were drawn exclusively from the ranks of the land-owning community. Proponents of the scheme included Henry George Grey (the third Earl Grey), Sir Walter Calverley Trevelyan, Sir John Swinburne, Sir Horace St Paul, George Annett Grey, John Ord, John Bolam, George Culley, and Thomas Mason.

Some of these gentlemen were prominent in national, as well as local life, and in this context it is interesting to record that Earl Grey (1802–1894) was the son of Charles Grey (1764–1865), the reforming Whig Prime Minister. Like his father, Henry George Grey was a leading Whig politician; he had been Secretary of State for the Colonies under Lord John Russell, and he later served in a Whig-Tory coalition government headed by the Earl of Derby. Although not as famous as Earl Grey, Sir Walter Calverley Trevelyan (1797–1879) was a noted geologist, and a cousin of Sir Charles Trevelyan, at one time the Permanent First Secretary of the Treasury and a powerful figure in mid-Victorian affairs.

All of the leading supporters lived locally, or had important interests in the central Northumberland area. Sir John Swinburne, for example, lived at Capheaton, near Scotsgap, while John Bolam resided at Alwinton, to the west of Rothbury. Several of the promoters lived in the Till Valley area around Wooler – among them George Culley of Fowberry, George Annett Grey of Milfield, and Sir Horace St Paul of Ewart Park; these gentlemen would have been well-known to each other, and it is easy to see how the concept of a 'Central Northumberland Railway' took firm root within this small, tightly-knit landowning community.

Although not a member of the 'county set' in the fullest sense of the term, Richard Hodgson was a neighbour of Messrs Bolam, Culley and St Paul – his country seat being situated at Carham, on the English side of the River Tweed, just 3 miles from Coldstream. As the chairman of a neighbouring railway company, he would clearly have been interested in any locally-inspired scheme, and it is hardly surprising that Mr Hodgson soon emerged as a pivotal figure during the planning of the Northumberland Central Railway.

John Furness Tone (1822-1881) was chosen as Engineer for the new railway. Born at Capheaton, Mr Tone was a local man who had started his career on the Newcastle & North Shields Railway. He later became Engineer to the Blyth & Tyne, Border Union and Wansbeck lines, and in 1862 he was commissioned to lay out the proposed 'Devon Central' lines from Exeter to Chagford, Okehampton and Torquay. Other work in south-western England followed, but Mr Tone was a Northumbrian, and although his West Country commissions were important, one feels that the Engineer was more than happy to lay-out the Northumberland Central Railway through his native county.

It was hoped that money for the proposed railway could be raised by the promoters themselves, the idea being that loans could be obtained from the Land Improvement Company on the assumption that railways were a means of increasing land values. This novel idea seemed, at the time, to offer a convenient solution to a variety of rural transport problems and, perhaps for this reason, the progress of the NCR scheme was fully reported in the pages of The Railway Times. On 14th February, 1863 this influential investors' journal printed a brief description of the system whereby the Northumberland Central promoters hoped to finance their 50 mile rural branch line:

> The landed interest are instructed by the proceedings of this company as to the method by which they may construct local lines without the intervention of speculators, and at the same time achieve independence for themselves in so far as existing systems are concerned. The scheme propounded by Mr Hodgson, as a landowner who appreciates the value conferred upon districts by railway accommodation, necessarily includes management as well as assessment and subscription. The scheme indeed can only be carried out where the landed gentry desire to retain control over their own property instead of its being cut up in a manner more suitable to the pecuniary advantage of contractors than to the efficient development of a district. Private security will thereby be thoroughly maintained while public interests are more vigorously prosecuted; and we sincerely trust that the landed gentry of the empire, who have been so much pestered of late by the intrusion of rival speculators, will now begin to act as well as to think for themselves.
>
> Meanwhile, let us desire success for the Northumberland Central as the pioneer of a new system under which branches may be profitably extended, and by which they can be kept as well as made feeders to the more expensive trunks that have done so much for the country, and in too many instances so little for their shareholders.

The paper then explained how, under the proposed system, property could be assessed for the purposes of obtaining a loan from the Land Improvement Company; landowners taking advantage of this system could then apply to the Enclosure Commissioners so that the intended loan could be charged upon their property. The conditions under which the Enclosure Commissioners could finally authorise the loan were as follows:

> The railway must have been completed and opened throughout for public traffic.
>
> The amount proposed to be charged must have been actually advanced and paid by the Lands Improvement Company to the landowner, or to the company, at his request.

The shares in the capital of the company subscribed for, or held by such landowner, or so many of such shares as are equal in nominal amount to the money advanced by the Lands Improvement Company, and authorised to be charged, must have been fully paid up in cash.

The certificates for the said paid-up shares, or for so many of them as will be equal in nominal amount to the money advanced by the Lands Improvement Company, and authorised to be charged upon the said lands, must be deposited by the landowner with the Enclosure Commissioners to be retained and held by them.

Commenting on the merits of this scheme, *The Railway Times* suggested that if further schemes could be financed 'on the security of rent-charges on land assessed in proportion to its estimated improved annual value', a 'great step would be gained towards perfect, as well as economic completion of the railway system in Great Britain'.

Having agreed that the Northumberland Central Railway was a viable proposition, Richard Hodgson, Earl Grey and the other promoters lost no time in putting their scheme into effect. At the same time, the Lands Improvement Company asked its agent to estimate the area of arable land which would benefit from the provision of a new rail link; it was suggested that 54,000 acres of arable and 'a large extent of grazing land' would be improved if the railway was built, the likely increased value of arable land being 2s. 6d. per acre, while grazing land would rise in value by around 6d. per acre. Although these estimates were moderate. Earl Grey and the other landowners were satisfied with the suggested figures which, if applied to the entire 54,000 acres between Scotsgap and Coldstream, would yield a net improvement value of £9,400.

The Scheme Proceeds

The publication and schedules of the proposed Northumberland Central Railway were dealt with by Messrs Pritt & Co., Parliamentary Agents, and plans and sections of the undertaking were deposited with the Clerk of the Peace for the County of Northumberland on 28th November, 1862. In February 1863 the promoters announced that 'Sir George Grey, Sir M.W. Ridley and Mr Hodgson' had consented to introduce the Bill, and a 'deposit of eight per cent on the estimated capital of £280,000' had been paid to the credit of the Accountant-General.

In an atmosphere of growing enthusiasm, the promoters held a further meeting at Morpeth in February 1863. Everything was, at this early stage, progressing smoothly, and the Northumberland Central supporters listened with considerable satisfaction as their Secretary, Mr Benjamin Woodman of Morpeth, read the following report:

> Your committee have used their best exertions to execute the duties intrusted to them since the general meeting at Morpeth on the 25th October, 1862 ... The answers returned to the notices on proprietors and occupiers comprise an unusually small proportion of dissents, and with the exception of one memorial against the Bill for non-compliance with the standing orders, opposition is practically wanting. This memorial is from the trustee of the Cornhill estate, which is held to be injuriously intersected by the Coldstream branch. If this objection could

be obviated, the committee are not without hope that the opposition on standing orders might be compromised.

The subscribers will remember that a pledge was given that up to the deposit of the Bill the whole expenses should not exceed £2,000, and as their solicitor and engineer offered to confine their charges to costs out of pocket until the Bill should become law, ... the committee have been able to redeem this pledge, and to reserve a portion of the guarantee fund in aid of further Parliamentary proceedings. It will remain for the subscribers now to determine whether the Bill shall progress, and in that event, to give definite authority to a small working committee, who shall have entire control of the Bill in its future stages.

The Secretary then referred to the accounts, a copy of which was appended to the report; there had, he said, been an expenditure of £1,893, but to meet this, £1,046 had been paid up in subscriptions, and a further £1,120 was 'in course of collection', leaving a balance of £247. The total expenditure to 4th February, 1863 was as follows:

Printing and advertising	£265
Parliamentary agents	£102
Engineering	£855
Plans	£333
Book of reference and other preliminary expenses	£287
Printing expenses and contingencies	£50
Grand total	£1,892

Alluding to the Land Improvement Company's assessment of a net improved annual value of £9,400 for lands served by the new railway, Mr Woodman intimated that 'the whole sum which might be raised on the estimated increased value per annum would be £141,000'. It was, he added, 'of the greatest moment . . . that the option of thus charging estates should be exercised, or agreed to be exercised, if Powers from Parliament be obtained'. Finally, the Secretary concluded with a note of caution:

It would be imprudent to prosecute the Bill through all its stages without, at the least, one half of the capital (or £130,000) being subscribed by one or other of these methods; but the committee have no reason to doubt that a much larger subscription may be obtained.

In order to withdraw the deposit (£20,800) from the custody of the Accountant-General on the passing of the said Act, it is requisite that a bond should be given by responsible persons for double that amount as security for one half the capital, at least, being expended under the Act; and it is obvious that no one will take the responsibility without the existence of a counter security afforded by a substantial proprietary of the company's shares. It is therefore proposed that the absolute control of the Bill, with power of withdrawal in the event of the subscriptions being inadequate . . . should be vested in those who may agree to give the bond in question, and thus put it in their power at any time to free themselves to the passing of the Act.

The next speaker was the redoubtable Richard Hodgson who, in moving the adoption of the report, claimed that he would not waste time by making any 'lengthy observations'. He then launched into a lengthy (and somewhat disingenuous) speech in which he strenuously denied that he was acting on behalf of the North British Railway! His interests in that railway were (he claimed) 'entirely separate and apart' from his involvement with the North-umberland Central, and he was not aware that the North British was in-terested in the Northumberland company 'in the slightest degree' – though there were hopes that the projected branch would be of benefit to the Wansbeck Railway, 'in which the North British had a pecuniary interest'. There were, he suggested, no reasons why the NBR should pay undue attention to the Northumberland Central, and indeed, the North British Directors 'would deny altogether that they had any interest or concern' in the undertaking.

Warming to his theme, Mr Hodgson proclaimed that it was as a landowner connected with the district that he supported the Northumberland Central, and he would, 'for the sake of the community', use his best exertions to 'obtain the success and progress' of the scheme. As a landowner he was prepared to support the proposed railway because, when opened, the new line would enable him to improve his property in various ways, and there would be a tangible, appreciable, and considerable' increase in the value of the estate. He would, for example, be able to 'communicate directly with districts from which he was now debarred, and would, by using the railway, be able to 'get things which he would not have got at a reasonable price before' and he believed that 'others would feel the advantage to a greater extent than he did himself'. He begged to say, therefore, that he would undertake to subscribe whatever amount might be necessary in order that the hoped-for railway could be built. He had heard it said that the proposed branch could only be made by the North British, North Eastern or other large companies, but (he argued) if they waited for the main line companies to build the line they 'would wait until Doomsday'; the only way in which the line would be built was if they did the job themselves – and that was, in any case, the best way! The line would 'necessarily pay a very high dividend', and if it could be constructed for the capital named – and he was assured by the Engineer that he had over-estimated the expense of the railway – he believed that it would pay 'ample remuneration to those who invested their money'.

Seconding the adoption of the report, Sir Horace St Paul agreed with Mr Hodgson that 'the Central Northumberland Railway was not only a public benefit but a public necessity'. An un-named landowner had told him that he would only support the railway when 'he perceived that it was a great public benefit', but he (Sir Horace) trusted that after the able address made by Mr Hodgson 'the gentlemen of the county' would learn to understand the true merits of the scheme. It had been said that Englishmen laughed at anything new, then 'raged at it', and then, having considered the matter, adopted the new idea; when their scheme was first propounded there were many among the upper classes who had laughed but now, he hoped, they were considering it, and after they had considered it he felt sure that 'both from the sense and good wishes of the public', they would give their full support.

Sir Horace added (pour encourager les autres) that the Land Improvement Company estimate for his own land was £140,000, but he was prepared to make an additional contribution of £70,000, representing a total of £210,000 for his own property. He had, furthermore, taken professional advice on the matter, and had 'received the opinion' that his estate would 'be benefited to the extent of £3,000'. He therefore agreed to take shares to that amount, and would 'stand the assessment' later. As a landowner he considered that the assessment was no great burden, but by buying Northumberland Central shares they would be making an even greater contribution to the scheme.

The report having been unanimously adopted, the promoters then discussed some general details relating to the proposed Scotsgap to Coldstream line. George Annett Grey stated that he would also be willing to submit to the assessment *and* subscribe for shares, while Mr Forster (an auditor) asked Mr Tone if the cost of the proposed Northumberland Central line would be greater or less than that of the recently completed Wansbeck Valley route; the Engineer answered without hesitation, and explained that the cost of the Wansbeck route had been 'rather less than £5,000 a mile, and that the new line was estimated to cost slightly more'.

The meeting ended with a further speech by Richard Hodgson, and having received a vote of thanks from the assembled promoters, the North British Chairman concluded the proceedings by wishing success for their new venture.

The Northumberland Central Act 1863

Meanwhile, the Northumberland Central Bill was progressing through the initial stages of its passage through Parliament, and in this context Richard Hodgson was once again able to play an important role. The success of the NCR Bill was never in doubt, and with much important landed support, the Bill 'for making Railways in the county of Northumberland from the Wansbeck Railway, in the parish of Hartburn, to the parish of Ford, and thence to the Berwick and Kelso Branch of the North Eastern Railway' received the Royal Assent on 28th July, 1863.

The resulting Act of Parliament (26 & 27 Vic. cap. 335) provided consent for the construction of a 49½ mile railway, which was carefully defined as a line:

> Commencing in the parish of Hartburn, in the county of Northumberland, by a junction with the Wansbeck Railway, and terminating in the parish of Ford, in the same county.

The above mentioned line was officially called 'the main line', and there was in addition, to be a short branch which was described as:

> A railway (hereinafter called the Cornhill Station Branch) from the main line at the Ford terminus thereof, to the Berwick and Kelso branch of the North Eastern Railway in the parish of Norham, in the same county.

Capital of £270,000 in ten pound shares was authorised, together with borrowing Powers for a further £90,000. The qualification for Directorship was set at £500, and the number of Directors would be nine. The Right Honourable the Earl Grey, Sir Walter Calverley Trevelyan, Baronet, George Annett Grey, Richard Hodgson MP, John Bolam, Thomas Mason and George Culley were mentioned by name as 'eight of the first Directors', and these individuals were to stay in office until the first ordinary meeting of the Northumberland Central company. At that meeting 'the shareholders present, either personally or by proxy' would be able to elect a new Board, or allow the original Directors 'to continue in office'.

Further provisions in the 1863 Act dealt with relations between the Northumberland Central Railway and neighbouring companies, and there were elaborate safeguards to prevent the Northumberland Central from infringing the rights of existing railways; one such provision warned that the Northumberland Central should not:

> In any manner, either permanently or temporarily, enter upon, take, or use any of the land or property of the North Eastern Railway Company, or in any manner alter, vary, or interfere with their Berwick and Kelso Branch, or any of the works appertaining thereto, save only so far as may be necessary for the purpose of constructing the Cornhill Station Branch thereto, as by this Act authorised and specially provided.

A similar provision was designed to safeguard the rights of the Wansbeck Railway at the southern end of the line, and this part of the Act stipulated that the Northumberland Central Railway should not:

> Take or enter upon any of the lands belonging to the Wansbeck Railway Company, or alter, vary, or interfere with the Wansbeck Railway, or any of the works thereof further or otherwise than is necessary for the construction of the railway hereby authorised and the convenient junction and intercommunication between the same and the Wansbeck Railway, without the consent, in writing, in every instance for that purpose.

Furthermore, the Act stated that plans of any junctions or works between the Wansbeck Railway and the authorised line 'should be submitted to the Engineer for the time being of the Wansbeck Railway Company' and in case of any difference arising in regard to such plans the matter would immediately be referred to the Board of Trade for arbitration.

Another part of the 1863 Act dealt with the erection of signals at the proposed junctions, and again, the Wansbeck and North Eastern companies were given wide-ranging powers. At the southern end of the line, for example, the Act provided that the Wansbeck Railway could:

> From time to time erect such signals and other works and conveniences and appoint and remove such watchmen, switchmen and other persons as that Company may deem necessary for the prevention of danger or obstruction to, or interference with, traffic at and near the junction between the railway hereby authorised and the Wansbeck Railway.

Moreover, the Act stipulated that the working and management of such 'signals, works and conveniences, and the reasonable wages of such watchmen, switchmen and other persons' would belong exclusively to the Wansbeck Railway – although their wages would, at the end of each half-year, be reinbursed by the Northumberland Central company. If the latter defaulted on these payments, 'the amount of such costs, expenses and wages' would be recovered by the Wansbeck Railway Company 'in any court of competent juristriction'.

In a more constructive vein, the Northumberland Central Act permitted the local company to enter into working agreements with 'the Wansbeck Railway, or the North Eastern Railway Company, and the North British Railway Company, or any one or more' of them. These agreements would relate to the following aspects of railway operation:

> The working, maintenance and use of the railways, or any of them or any part thereof respectively, and of the works or any of them connected therewith.
>
> The supply of engines, carriages and rolling stock for the purposes of the railways.
>
> The conduct, regulation, interchange and management of the traffic in or upon or over the railways or any of them or any part thereof respectively.
>
> The affording of facilities for the transfer and transmission of traffic passing to and from the railways of the Companies parties to the agreement, and the conveyance of such traffic over all or any of such railways.
>
> The fixing, levying, dividing and apportioning of tolls and charges arising from such trains.
>
> The appointment of joint committees and the powers to be conferred on such committees.
>
> The modification of any agreement previously entered into.

Having obtained their Act, the promoters were able to organise themselves into a properly-constituted Board of Directors. Earl Grey was an obvious choice as Northumberland Central Chairman, while most of the provisional Directors mentioned in the 1863 Act remained on the NCR Board during the formative years of the company.

The Northumberland Central Railway was never short of Directors, and the rapidity with which the 9-man Board was formed illustrates the very real enthusiasm of the promoters. Although the NCR Board was destined to undergo at least one major reshuffle, the original promoters were a distinct and readily-identifiable body; the Directors of the NCR company, on the eve of construction, were as follows:

Earl Grey (Chairman)	John Bolam	John Ord
Sir Horace St Paul	Richard Hodgson	George Culley
Sir John Swinburne	George Annett Grey	Sir Walter Calverley Trevelyan

Others involved with the scheme during the early 1860s included Secretary Benjamin Woodward (a Morpeth solicitor) and Auditors William Forster and Thomas Gow; the line's Engineer was, of course, John Furness Tone.

As we shall see, Mr Tone was not allowed to complete his work on the Northumberland Central line, while William Forster (Junior) and Thomas Gow later joined the Board as Directors. These changes were, however, in the future, and what mattered in 1864, was that the Act had been obtained, and at least some money was starting to flow in; the Northumberland Central project had made a good start, and those concerned with the scheme had every reason to believe that their 50 mile-long railway from Scotsgap to Cornhill was about to become a reality.

A turn-of-the-century commercial postcard view of Thrum Mill near Rothbury.
Oakwood Collection

An early postcard view of Rothbury terminus showing clearly the use of the turntable as a three way point. The wooden locomotive shed stands on the right. *Lens of Sutton*

AN

A C T

For making Railways in the county of Northumberland from the Wansbeck Railway, in the parish of Hartburn, to the parish of Ford, and thence to the Berwick and Kelso Branch of the North-Eastern Railway; and for other purposes.

[ROYAL ASSENT, 28TH JULY, 1863.]

WHEREAS a railway from the Wansbeck Railway, in the parish of Preamble Hartburn, in the county of Northumberland, to the parish of Ford, in the same county, with branch railways therefrom, to the Berwick and Kelso branch of the North Eastern Railway, in the parish of Norham, would be of great public and local advantage, especially to the proprietors in and near to the line of the proposed railways.

The opening sentences of the 1863 Act for the Rothbury Branch.

A class 'G5' 0–4–4T No. 67295 hurries along the branch near Scotsgap Junction with its one-coach train. In earlier years, cattle wagons were often attached to passenger workings.   *E.E. Smith*

A fine view of the turntable, locomotive shed and water tower (and a locomctive taking on water) at Rothbury terminus. Note the turntable locking-rod running from the signal box and that the locomotive shed is now brick-built as compared to the view on page 18.

E.E. Smith, courtesy Neville Stead

Chapter Two

Construction, Opening and Early Years (1863–1880)

The authorised route of the Northumberland Central Railway followed a circuitous, though generally easy course between the Cheviots and the sea. Commencing at an elevation of approximately 500 ft near Scotsgap, the route climbed steeply towards Longwitton before dropping abruptly into the Coquet Valley. Descending to around 380 ft at Rothbury, the suggested route continued along the Coquet Valley towards Thropton before turning northwards along a subsidiary valley to Alnham. Having surmounted an intervening ridge of higher land around Alnham, the northwards path continued along the Breamish Valley via Glanton, Wooperton, and Ilderton. Beyond, the low-lying valley of the River Till provided an obvious route for the remainder of the line to Cornhill.

With an average elevation of about 125–150 ft, the northern section of the Northumberland Central line would traverse a prosperous agricultural area, and the scheme's supporters hoped that stations established at Wooler, Milfield (and elsewhere) would generate significant agricultural traffic. Indeed, the northern half of the Northumberland Central line was perhaps the most important section of the entire scheme in that it presented few engineering problems, while promising to be the most lucrative section of the projected railway.

The Problems Begin

The line was staked out ready for construction by the early months of 1864, and on 20th February the Directors announced that negotations for the purchase of land had 'progressed'. Terms had been arranged for the acquisition 'of all the land required for the line from Rothbury to its junction with the Wansbeck', while similar progress had been made with land purchases 'for several miles at the northern end'. However, the Directors reported that little capital had been subscribed, and they warned that 'in the event of the deficiency not being supplied' they would be able to proceed only with the southernmost section of line between Scotsgap and Rothbury – a distance of just 13 miles.

Further problems ensued when the contractors (Messrs Waring) refused to commence the works, and with only £55,000 available to begin construction, the Directors agreed – after some internal arguments – that it would be impossible 'to begin both ends at once'.

It was becoming clear to all concerned that the grandly-named Northumberland Central Railway could not be built in its entirety, and in these circumstances the NCR Directors were probably right in their decision to amend the scheme. What is perhaps surprising in the way in which attention immediately focussed on the southern part of the route; as mentioned above, the northern section of the line appeared to have considerable traffic potential, whereas the portion from Scotsgap to Rothbury traversed an under-populated moorland area which seemed, at first glance, to offer little scope for the development of passenger or freight traffic. Moreover, many of the Northumberland Central supporters lived, not in the Rothbury area but along the northern part of the projected route, and there is no doubt that people such as Sir Horace St Paul and George Annett Grey would have favoured an early commencement of the Till Valley line between Wooler and Cornhill.

A clue to the Directors' curious behaviour at this time may be found in the ambiguous attitude of neighbouring main line companies. In theory, the completed Northumberland Central scheme could have formed a useful link between the North British Railway at Scotsgap and the North Eastern system at Coldstream, but in reality these two companies did not necessarily want a jointly-owned link between Scotsgap and Coldstream. The North British may indeed have welcomed an opportunity to penetrate North Eastern territory, but at the same time the NBR did *not* want the North Eastern to extend its own influence southwards to Scotsgap. Thus the North British, while actively supporting a short branch to Rothbury, may not have wanted the Northumberland Central to reach its ultimate objective on 'the Berwick & Kelso branch of the North Eastern Railway', and given that the NCR promoters were (because of Richard Hodgson) associated with the NBR, the decision to build the Scotsgap to Rothbury section can perhaps be explained. For his part, Mr Hodgson remained firmly committed to the original scheme for a line from Scotsgap to Coldstream, but at the same time the North British Chairman could not act without the support of his fellow NBR Directors – and as we shall see, the North British soon adopted an ambivalent attitude towards the entire Northumberland Central project.

An Important Meeting

With problems mounting on all sides, the Northumberland Central Directors continued to press their land-owning neighbours for financial support, but interest seems to have decreased after the initial failure to begin construction, and the half-year meeting held at Alnwick in August 1865 was a sombre gathering. The meeting was chaired by Earl Grey, and the proceedings were fully reported by *The Railway Times*:

> The Chairman, in moving adoption of the report, said that he was sorry he could not congratulate the meeting on a more favourable state of the affairs of the company. Undoubtedly there had been various circumstances which had arisen to cause regret. In the first place, he regretted that the differences that had arisen with the contractors had hitherto prevented the commencement of the works; but the Directors were not responsible for the delay.
>
> They had done all in their power to induce the contractors to proceed with the works, and having failed in that they had now to take the best course that remained open to them. But he still more regretted that the absence of greater support from landowners on the projected lines, with the loss also of the assistance of the Messrs Waring, made it impossible for the Directors to recommend to them that they should proceed to construct the railway at both ends simultaneously. He deeply regretted that, because he was aware how strong a desire existed among a very great body of the shareholders that the work should be begun at both ends, and that desire he fully shared; but, as practical men, they must consider what was the course which was really best for them in the circumstances in which they were placed – in what manner they could best proceed so as to afford the best prospect of accomplishing the railway as originally intended.

It was clear, repeated the Chairman, that the scheme had been 'blighted' by those landowners who had failed to support the proposed railway; he thought that they had a right to *expect* that support because everybody agreed on 'the extreme importance of railway communication'. It was quite clear, he added, that:

> Those districts that did not possess the advantages of railway communication were exposed to a more and more unfavourable position compared with those districts that did possess it, and there was no district in the country in which that disadvantage was more felt than in that through which their projected railway would pass, and he might say there was hardly any that would derive greater benefit from the construction of a line, because it would bring together two parts of a district, in one of which coal and lime were abundant, and in the other deficient, and so it would be to the mutual advantage of both. If proper pains were taken by the shareholders, he felt convinced that ultimately they would make the whole line.
>
> Undoubtedly, at present their capital was far short of that purpose, but they had funds sufficient to enable them to construct the line from Scots Gap to Rothbury, and that was what the Directors proposed doing. He was quite aware that there were many gentlemen averse to the arrangement, and who thought it would be much more desirable to begin both ends at once. Now if there had been money enough to have completed the two sections as proposed he, for one, would have adhered to the original project, and would have concurred in that opinion. But, abandoned as they had been by Messrs Waring, deprived of the assistance of those gentlemen, and left entirely to their own resources, he thought the case was very doubtful, and it seemed to him to be highly impolitic, seeing that they had so small an amount of money at their disposal, that they should divide that money and commence spending it at both ends.

Concluding his report, the Chairman stressed that it was of supreme importance that the proprietors should show 'some confidence in their Directors'. They were faced with an uphill struggle in 'trying to push on the enterprise with the lukewarm support they had received, and unless they were to have the support of the shareholders in acting on the policy which, on full and deliberate consideration, they believed to be the best, he was sure that the sooner they relieved them from their exceedingly difficult and irksome duties the better'.

With this thinly-veiled threat to resign from the Board, the Chairman sat down. The report was then seconded by Sir John Swinburne, but the next speaker – Sir Horace St Paul – challenged the decision to begin construction only at one end. While regretting that it was 'extremely painful to him to be standing there in some measure advocating opinions differing from his brother Directors', Sir Horace – who lived on the northern section of the proposed line – suggested that what little money was available should be expended on the northern part of the route:

> It was perfectly true they had not sufficient funds by half to accomplish the two sections. The southern section would cost about £70,000, the northern about £35,000, making together about £100,000. To accomplish that they had about £55,000. They would observe that the present proposition of the Directors was to begin at the most expensive end – £70,000 against £35,000. One important reason, therefore, for beginning the northern division first was that it was cheapest to

construct both in amount and per mile. Another reason, and a most important one, was that they depended on public payments, and they might rely on this – that if they left the northern division in the lurch they would certainly lose public favour.

Having made out a convincing case for building the northern half of the line, Sir Horace proposed an amendment to the effect that the works should be commenced at *both* ends. Further discussion ensued, and there was as a result a suggestion that, although the southern section would be built first, this course of action would not preclude the construction of the northern section at a later date. This compromise solution was advocated by Mr Hodgson, who proposed the following double motion:

> 1) That in assenting to the construction of the southern section, this meeting disclaims any intention of abandoning the other parts. On the contrary, they would hold the company bound to proceed as early as circumstances will permit, with the construction of the whole of the line, and specially with the northern section from Cornhill to Wooler.
> 2) That as soon as the southern section is opened for traffic it will be expedient to endeavour to raise funds for the completion of the northern section, by the issue, if necessary, of any preference shares.

On being put to the meeting the first motion was carried unanimously, while the second was defeated by nine votes to five. The meeting was ended by Earl Grey, who considered that the resolution they had reached 'was a wholesome one'; he thought that, with the support they had received, they would be able to push on the railway 'and bring it to a successful termination'.

Further Difficulties

The August 1865 NCR meeting was of considerable importance in that it enabled the Directors to clarify their objectives and obtain renewed support from the proprietors. Unfortunately, the decision to commence work only on the Rothbury section was not in itself sufficient to rescue the company, and the underlying problem – that is to say lack of money – could not easily be solved. Nevertheless, the amended scheme was put into effect, and on 10th March, 1866 *The Railway Times* was able to print the following progress report:

> NORTHUMBERLAND CENTRAL – The half-yearly meeting was held at Alnwick on 28th ultimate; Mr Richard Hodgson in the chair. The report, which was adopted, stated that contracts for the construction of the section of the railway from Scot's Gap to Rothbury had been let for the aggregate sum of £44,498 exclusive of materials for the permanent way. The whole of the land on this section had been obtained for an annual rent-charge in lieu of purchase, thus leaving the subscribed capital available for the construction of that portion of the line which it was expected would be open for traffic in about twelve months. Sir J. Swinburn, Mr R. Hodgson and Mr G.A. Grey, the retiring Directors, were re-elected; and also Mr W. Foster the retiring auditor.

It seemed that, in the Spring of 1866, some progress might at last be made, but in May 1866 the sudden failure of bankers Overend & Gurney threw the whole Victorian financial system into chaos. The government was forced to suspend the Bank Charter Act and panic shook the City; for three months the bank rate stood at a crippling 10 per cent, and with individuals and companies facing ruin small companies such as the Northumberland Central Railway were unable to raise their authorised capital. For the already-impoverished NCR the crisis came as a body blow, and in these melancholy conditions the scheme almost foundered.

The failure of Overend & Gurney was, by any definition, a major problem for the Northumberland Central supporters, but the crisis of May 1866 led, in turn, to an event of comparable magnitude – a catastrophe which came close to destroying the NCR in its entirety.

The central player in the 1866 crisis was, as so often in Northumberland Central affairs, none other than Richard Hodgson. As we have seen, Mr Hodgson had played a crucial role during the promotion of the NCR, his role in Northumberland Central politics being underlined by his position as Chairman of the North British Railway. Indeed, the Northumberland Central was just one of series of NBR-backed lines on the English side of the border which, between them, carried North British influence well beyond its undisputed heartland in the Edinburgh Lowlands.

All of these 'English' lines were, in great part, linked with Richard Hodgson's vision of a greater North British Railway which would straddle both sides of the border and openly challenge the rival North Eastern and Caledonian companies for control over a vast tract of countryside between the Tyne and the Tay. Sadly, these grandiose schemes were not appreciated by the North British shareholders – many of whom feared (with justification) that the company would dissipate its energies in pointless wars with the NER and Caledonian railways.

Opposition to Richard Hodgson had become particularly strong among certain NBR proprietors who, with typical Scottish perspicacity, felt that the company should be carefully managed so as to ensure maximum dividends for minimal financial risk. Such views were well-suited to the needs of small investors, but they were diametrically opposed to Mr Hodgson's flamboyant style of management! There could be no compromise between the NBR Chairman and his vociferous critics, and when the 1866 financial crisis exposed the weakness of the Chairman's position his enemies struck with overwhelming force. The unfortunate Mr Hodgson was accused of financial irregularities, the resulting furore being so great that – after a long and bitter struggle – Richard Hodgson was forced to retire. His actual resignation did not take place until the end of the year, but in the meantime the Chairman's position had rapidly become untenable, and it soon became clear that the Northumberland Central promoters were about to be abandoned by their NBR allies.

Richard Hodgson was by the Autumn of 1866, a sick and broken man; his enemies were triumphant on every front, and in these circumstances it was obvious that the NCR promoters would soon have few friends north of the border. Rothbury was, after all, a long way from Edinburgh, and in a period of financial stringency there was little incentive for the post-Hodgson North British Board to underwrite the operations of an obscure Northumbrian branch line when they were unable to pay a dividend on their own ordinary shares. Moreover, the Northumberland Central scheme was closely identified with Richard Hodgson's expansionist policies, and this was more than enough to condemn the scheme in the wake of Hodgson's spectacular fall from power.

To their credit the Northumberland Central Directors refused to be intimidated by the North British defection and the underlying economic crisis – after all, great magnates such as Earl Grey owned their wealth, not to the capitalist system but to land; they were, in a very real sense, the representatives of 'old wealth', and although the 1866 financial crisis was a major blow, the NCR supporters (or at least some of them) felt that the scheme should be seen through to a conclusion – with or without North British support.

There were renewed efforts to raise capital and sustain support among the landowning community, and the Northumberland Central Directors were able to persuade more of their friends and neighbours that the scheme was still worthwhile. In October 1866, for example, a 'large and influential gathering' was held in Rothbury, and several new members were added to the committee that had been appointed to 'treat with landowners'; these new men included 'Mr Selby, Sir W. Riddell, Mr W. Wilkinson, Sir W. Armstrong and Mr G.D. Wealleans'.

Sadly, the enlarged committee failed to sway those landowners who had stubbornly and persistently withheld their support for the NCR, and the Northumberland Central Directors reluctantly agreed that their scheme would never be raised above branch line status. In recognition of this sad state of affairs, the company prepared another Bill for submission to Parliament, and on 12th April, 1867 they obtained an Act to authorise the formal abandonment of the northern part of the Northumberland Central route. At the same time, the company's capital was reduced from £270,000 to £75,000, while borrowing Powers were reduced from £90,000 to just £25,000.

It was hoped that the Scotsgap to Rothbury line could be completed for relatively little outlay, and in 1869 Mr Tone suggested (perhaps optimistically) that he would be able to finish the branch within a budget of around £40,000. Meanwhile, the continued difficulties experienced by the hapless Northumberland Central promoters had resulted in major differences of opinion within the company – these problems being worsened by a split between Richard Hodgson and some of the other NCR Board members. The ramifications of this split were complex (and of little interest to the general reader), though it may be worth noting that Mr Hodgson's increasingly isolated position vis-à-vis his fellow NCR Directors had at least one long term effect on the future Northumberland Central Railway. It seems that John Furness Tone was an associate of Mr Hodgson and, perhaps for this reason, he was dismissed by the NCR Board. In his place they appointed George Barclay Bruce of 2 Westminster Chambers, Westminster, and this new engineer thereby became identified with the anti-Hodgson faction on the Northumberland Central Board.

Mr Tone's dismissal was, to say the least, a curious action for the Board to have taken. John Furness Tone was a local man of great experience, not only on local lines such as the Border Counties line and the Wansbeck Valley

Railway but also on projects in the West of England. He had been associated with the Northumberland Central from its very inception, and the manner of his dismissal (when Mr Hodgson was abroad) did little to ease tensions within the NCR Board.

In the meantime, the Northumberland Central promoters were still struggling to raise sufficient capital to resume construction, and in August 1869 it was announced that the Directors had re-let the works and were endeavouring 'to ensure, with due regard to economy, the early completion of the line from Scots Gap to Rothbury'. Sadly, the original contractor had initiated legal proceedings in an attempt to recover a sum of money that he claimed was owed for alleged breach of contracts that he had entered into with the Northumberland Central Railway.

Construction Proceeds

With construction at last under way, the Scotsgap to Rothbury line began to take tangible shape in the bleak Northumberland hills. On 25th August, 1869, Mr Bruce estimated that the cost of construction would be £49,411 inclusive of liabilities due at that time; in an attempt to reduce already escalating costs, he proposed to introduce steeper gradients than those envisaged by Mr Tone. Costs nevertheless continued to rise, and Bradshaw's Shareholders Manual told potential investors that NCR expenditure for the first half of 1869 had been as follows:

CAPITAL: The expenditure to 30th June had been £52,585, of which £9,689 took place in the last half-year, the two chief items being £6,107 to contractors and £1,804 for engineering. It was estimated that £26,100 would be expended during the half-year ending 31st December, 1869, and in the subsequent half-year, £8,400. To meet this further expenditure there is share and loan capital to the amount of £42,448 authorised or created, but not yet received.

On a more optimistic note, it was reported that the NCR Company had obtained an injunction to restrain Messrs Waring from proceeding with their action for alleged breach of contract – and the contractors had been advised that they had no valid claim against the Northumberland Central Railway.

With the Rothbury branch nearing completion, the NCR Directors turned their attention to operational matters. There was no thought of working their own line, but the Northumberland Central supporters were still confident that the North British would willingly work the completed NCR in return for token payments in respect of fuel, staff and rolling stock. However, the North British was determined that the NCR should pay the true costs of working the line, and the Northumberland Central Directors were left in no doubt that, whatever agreements were eventually concluded between the two companies, the arrangements would now be made on a strictly business basis.

Unable (or perhaps unwilling) to accept that the North British would not work the Rothbury branch for a pittance, the Northumberland Central Directors took the unusual step of sending a copy of the incomplete working agreement to the Board of Trade. The suggested agreement (which had not been signed by the NBR) stated that the North British Company would

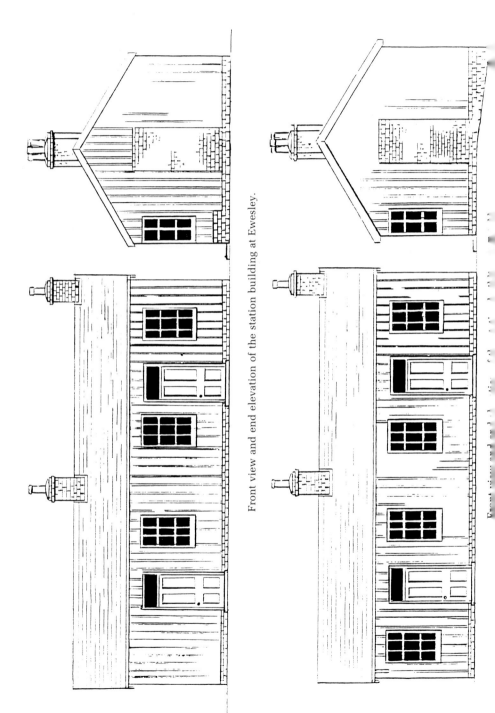

Front view and end elevation of the station building at Ewesley.

'provide an engine for the working of the Northumberland Central Railway at a cost of eleven pence per mile – the minimum number of miles being 78 per diem'. In return for this modest payment the NCR expected the North British to provide both stores and fuel for the locomotive, plus the entire wages of a driver, fireman and cleaner. In addition, it was hoped that the North British would furnish 'such number of passenger carriages and brake vans' as the Northumberland Central would require for the proper working of their line. As if these terms were not generous enough, the Northumberland Central Directors anticipated that the NBR train crews would be deemed 'servants of the Northumberland Central Company'. At Scotsgap, the NCR would pay £50 rent and tolls for use of the station and junction facilities, while maintenance would be 'in accordance with the Act of Parliament – viz, cost price to be charged against the Northumberland Central'. The proposed working agreement would last for 12 months in the first instance, with 3 months notice on either side.

The Northumberland Central Board may have hoped that, by sending their proposed agreement to the Board of Trade, they would gain official sanction. If this was in fact the case, the NCR ploy was a total failure, and in a swift counter-move the North British tersely informed the Board of Trade that, as far as they were concerned, the NCR would be working its own line! Chastened, the Northumberland Central representatives resumed negotiations with their North British counterparts, the resulting working agreement being (in the words of a NCR Director) 'all favourable to the working company and all unfavourable to themselves as constructors'.

In June 1870 the NCR Directors called a special meeting at Newcastle, the object of this gathering being – as usual – the need to raise sufficient capital to complete the works. It was resolved that shares and debentures to the value of £6,500 would be created to complete the line, the said shares being 'issued and distributed rateably among the persons or person making the advance'. It was expected that the railway would be opened to traffic within the next few weeks, but in the event this prediction was slightly optimistic, and public services did not start until the following November.

The Northumberland Central line was, nevertheless, substantially complete by the summer of 1870, and after many setbacks, the supporters of the troubled scheme could, at long last, see their railway taking tangible shape amid the Northumberland hills.

The line itself was formed of a makeshift assortment of permanent way materials that at least had the advantage of cheapness; most of the track was formed of relatively lightweight 60 lb. per yard single-headed rail resting on roughly-hewn cross sleepers that had probably been acquired locally, while many overbridges were of timber construction. Stations, too, were cheaply-built of timber – economic considerations being of paramount importance to the Northumberland Central Directors. (There were, in addition to the terminus at Rothbury, three intermediate stopping places, though only two were ready for use at the time of opening.)

The Board of Trade Inspection

It was necessary, before the line could be opened for public traffic, for the route to be inspected by a Board of Trade inspector, and the NCR Directors therefore wrote to the BoT to say that the new line was ready for opening. In reply, the Board of Trade informed the NCR that the branch would be inspected by Lt Colonel C. Hutchinson in the following September.

Unfortunately, the NCR line was not quite ready in time for the inspection, the main problems being around the mid-point of the line where the route crossed the rivers Fontburn and Forestburn on a large viaduct and a small culvert respectively; the embankments on this part of the line had shown a distressing tendency to slip, and as he carefully scrutinised the new works Lt Colonel Hutchinson immediately identified a source of danger. Unhappy with what he had seen, the BoT inspector produced a mildly critical report, and this document is worth quoting in full:

21st September, 1870

Sir,

In compliance with the instructions contained in your minute of the 12th instant, I have the honour to report, for the information of the Board of Trade, that I have inspected the Northumberland Central Railway.

This line runs from Scots Gap station, on the Wansbeck Valley branch of the North British Railway, to Rothbury. The original project was to have extended it to Coldstream on the Kelso and Tweedsmouth branch of the North Eastern Railway, but the portion between Rothbury and Coldstream has been abandoned by Act of Parliament.

This line is nearly 13 miles long and is single throughout, with sidings at three of the stations, viz Ewesley, Brinkburn and Rothbury; the fourth, Rothley, has only a platform and booking office. The gauge is 4 ft 8½ in., and there is an interval of 6 ft between the lines where there is more than one. Land has been purchased for a double line, but the works are all constructed for only a single line of rails.

The permanent way consists of single headed rails weighing 60 lb. to the yard laid on transverse sleepers at central intervals of 3 ft. The rails are secured to the sleepers for the most part by fang bolts and partly by dog spikes. They are fished at the joints. The sleepers are, for the most part, half round, and measure 9 ft by 9 in. by 4½ inches. The ballast is of broken stone and gravel and is stated to have a depth of 15 inches beneath the underside of the sleepers.

The steepest gradient on the line has an inclination of 1 in 60, and the sharpest curve a radius of 15¾ chains . . . There are 26 bridges under the line and 16 over it . . . The largest span of an underbridge is 31 ft, and of an overbridge 20½ ft. There is also a viaduct of twelve masonry spans of 30 ft over the River Font, and there are six large culverts under the line.

All these works appear to be substantially constructed, are standing well, and appear to have sufficient theoretical and practical strength, with the exception of a large culvert at 7 miles 40 chains, which passes through a heavy bank. This has considerably changed in form, and will require careful and constant watching. The bank itself has slipped considerably from time to time, and though it appears to be tolerably stable, it will also need constant watching during the coming winter, and I should recommend that a very slow speed be insisted on in passing over it.

The fencing is for the most part of post and rail, with occasional portions of dry stone wall. There are no tunnels and no level crossings on the line. I observed the following requirements during the inspection.

1) Scotsgap Station: The facing points for trains approaching from Morpeth to be locked right for such trains by the signals when taken off. Shelter required on the platform.

2) Planking on 2 cast iron bridges requires coarsing with ballast. Some holding down bolts required in the longitudinal timbers on the bridge at 4 miles 35 chains.

3) Bad joint in rail at about 4 miles 50 chains requires making good, and some additional spikes required in a crossing at Brinkburn station.

No definite arrangements have yet been concluded as to the mode of working the line, and pending the completion of the above named requirements, and upon the receipt of a satisfactory undertaking as to the mode of working the line, I must report that, by reason of the incompleteness of the works, the Northumberland Central Railway cannot be opened for passenger traffic without danger to the public using the same.

> I have the honour to remain, Sir,
> Your most obedient servant,
> C.S. Hutchinson,
> Lt Colonel

The inspector's decision, though harsh, was hardly unexpected. The Northumberland Central Engineer was instructed to rectify the various deficiencies at Scotsgap and elsewhere, and after a week of frantic work on the line, he was able to write to Lt Colonel Hutchinson on 27th September, telling him that the bridge works had been completed, loose stones had been removed from rock cuttings, and other unfinished details had been put into a state of order. However, added the NCR Engineer, the working agreement with the North British Railway had still not been finalised, and he ended his letter in a pleading manner:

> I am afraid that the working agreement with the North British Railway has not yet been completed, but if it is consistent with your usual mode of acting I should be glad of a certificate allowing us to open the line subject to the receipt of the North British assent to the system of working.

George Barclay Bruce's reference to the 'usual mode of acting' of the Board of Trade suggests that he was unfamiliar with the procedures to be followed before railways could be opened, and this impression was reinforced when, at around the same time, the NCR company informed the BoT that the branch would be worked on the 'one-engine-in-steam' system. It appears that the Northumberland Central Directors did not know what this phrase actually meant, because the Company Secretary subsequently wrote to Lt Colonel Hutchinson asking if 'one-engine-in-steam' could be construed as two locomotives coupled together at the head of one train. The Lt Colonel must, by this stage, have realised that the Northumberland Central proprietors were complete amateurs as far as railways were concerned, and he sent them a brief explanation of how 'one-engine-in-steam' meant one engine or two coupled together hauling one train on a single line. Meanwhile, the unco-operative attitude displayed by the North British Railway towards its tiny protégé had moderated slightly, and the Board of Trade being satisfied by George Barclay Bruce's letter, the very first trains were apparently run on 8th October, 1870.

Opening of the Railway

Having passed its obligatory Board of Trade inspection, the Scotsgap to Rothbury branch was ceremonially opened to public traffic on Tuesday 1st November, 1870. The event was celebrated in the usual way, with glowing speeches in the Rothbury Hotel – though after the trials and tribulations of the previous seven years, the Northumberland Central supporters no doubt felt they deserved the luxury of a modest celebration! The event was reported in local papers, and also in *The Railway Times* which, on 5th November, 1870, printed the following brief report:

> NORTHUMBERLAND CENTRAL – The first section of this line, from Scot's Gap to Rothbury, was formally opened for traffic on Tuesday. The length of line was 12 miles. The cost of the works was much more than originally expected, but after considerable delay, and by the aid of the Duke of Northumberland, the above section was at length completed. The event was celebrated at the Rothbury Hotel, Earl Percy presiding at the dinner, and a ball in the evening concluded the proceedings.

A much fuller report appeared in the *Newcastle Daily Journal* within hours of the opening ceremony, and this more detailed version of the Great Day is worth quoting in some detail. The paper reported that 'a large party, consisting of the shareholders, directors and officials of the company' had travelled over the line in a special train, a 'great number of invitations' having been previously sent out to the leading gentlemen and landowners of the district. The special left Morpeth at 10.00 am, and after arrival at Rothbury the invited guests 'dispersed over the beautiful scenery with which the locality abounds, and also visited the romantic grounds of Cragside Hall, the country seat of Sir William Armstrong, which had been kindly thrown open to visitors'. The report continued as follows:

> The luncheon at the Rothbury Hotel took place at two o'clock; and an admirable repast was served up by Mr English, the manager of the hotel, assisted by Mr Liddell, of Gateshead, who had been called in for the occasion.
>
> The chair was occupied by the Right Hon. Earl Percy, MP, and the vice-chairs by Mr J. Ord, Nesbitt, Kelso, and Mr J. Dodd Wealleans, Flotterton; and amongst those present were – Mr C.W. Orde, Mr H. Riddell, Captain Ilderton, Mr William Forster, Mr Joseph Snowball, the Reverend G. West, Mr McPhearson, Dr Bruce, Mr N. Wright, Mr Hood (Mayor of Morpeth), Miss Robson, Dr Richardson, Mr Jacob Wilson, Mr S. Holmes (resident engineer), Mr B. Woodman, Mr Jobson, Mr E. Mather, Mr W. Anderson, Mr Barry, Mr W. Grey, the Hon. and Rev. Mr Ellis, and Mrs Ellis, Mr E. Pringle, Mr Clennel, Mrs Waddilove, the Reverend G.S. Thompson, Mr George Bruce (engineer for the line), Mr Bell (North British Company), Mr John Pattinson, Mr Thomas Ord, Mr J. Hunter, Mr J. Ronaldson, Mr Colville, Mr J.O. Sturgeon, Mr J.S. Challoner, Mr M. Lambert, Mr Dowson, Mr George Wilson, Ald. Duncan.
>
> The cloth having been removed, the noble Chairman proposed 'The Queen', 'The Prince and Princess of Wales and the rest of the Royal Family', and 'The Bishop and Clergy of the Diocese and the Ministers of all Denominations' – The Rev. G. West responded.
>
> The Chairman next proposed, 'The Army, Navy and Volunteers' – Colonel Brumell, 3rd Northumberland Rifles (Morpeth) responded.

The Chairman next proposed 'The Lord-Lieutenant and the Magistrates of the County'. His Lordship said that the Lord-Lieutenant set an example, and the magistrates followed him, in showing great interest in this county in all that affects the welfare of its inhabitants. Of that, he thought that the railway they had that day opened as a very good instance. Without enlarging upon these points, which no doubt were as well known to his hearers as to himself, he should content himself with coupling with the toast the name of a gentleman who holds a prominent rank among the magistrates of the county, and who he believed was highly esteemed by every one who knew him, and who was interested greatly in that railway inasmuch as it cuts through a great deal of his land; he referred to Mr Orde.

Mr C.W. Orde, Nunnykirk, Chairman of the Quarter Sessions, responded. He said, highly flattered as he was by the manner in which the noble Earl had proposed his health, he must not forget that a higher duty devolved upon him – that of acknowledging the health of the distinguished nobleman who fills the office of Lord-Lieutenant of the county. He did not know to what extent the Lord-Lieutenant was interested in this undertaking, but he knew his Grace took great interest in the railway, and he would hear with great pleasure that the railway up the valley of Rothbury had been opened to the public. With respect to himself, he felt excessively obliged. It had devolved upon him for many years to return thanks for the magistrates, but it was a new circumstance to have the Lord Lieutenant combined with the toast; but he believed that in these days the rapidity with which things went required the amalgamation of toasts to an extent not before known (applause).

The Chairman said he now found it his duty to propose the toast of the evening – 'The Northumberland Central Railway, the health of the chairman, Sir Walter Trevelyan, and the Board of Directors, and prosperity to the undertaking'. He thought he was justified in saying they had opened this railway under the very happiest auspices they could expect. They had had fine weather, a great concourse of spectators from all sides to do honour for the occasion, and showing thereby how widespread and heartfelt were the wishes for its prosperity. He need scarcely say that he joined very heartily in those good wishes. He trusted that prosperity would attend the undertaking, and that it might tend to the advantage of the shareholders, the inhabitants of the district, and the public. Running as it does through a district not very thickly inhabited, the railway would probably have to trust to a great extent to its traffic other than passengers. At the same time, he was led to hope, by the beautiful scenery it opens up and by the character which that place bears for healthiness, by the fact that that place had of late become the place of resort for many, and looking now to that building in which they were assembled, he said he was led by these things to hope that there might be a good deal of passenger traffic along the line, and he hoped that the line would be so worked as to afford the greatest amount of convenience to all the different classes likely to use it.

The next speaker was John Ord an NCR Director, who, with Sir Walter Calverley Trevelyan, had loyally supported the Northumberland Central Railway throughout the many vicissitudes of the 1860s. Sir Walter was unable to attend the opening Day ceremonies, but as the 'senior director present', Mr Ord was well able to speak on behalf of the NCR company. Having apologised for Sir Walter's unavoidable absence, Mr Ord thanked Earl Grey, the Duke of Northumberland, 'and one or two others who were not now connected with the company' who had liberally supported the project during its greatest difficulties. In reflective mood, Mr Ord told his listeners that he was about to relinquish his associations with the Rothbury area:

> He regretted that, in a few days, his connections as a landed proprietor in the county of Northumberland would cease. But the recollections of the county would not cease because of an old maternal ancestral property passing from him; and whatever his future in life might be cast, he should ever remember the many kind friends whom he had made in Northumberland. He would never forget the grassy slopes and the heathery hills, and silver streams of Coquetdale. (Applause). He had now a pleasing duty to perform. He had been asked to offer for their acceptance as a toast the health of a nobleman distinguished for his many amiable qualities, and for the active part he had taken in every matter connected with the prosperity of the county of Northumberland. His Grace's many good qualities were probably better known to them than to himself; but he knew that if called upon in the interests of his large estates, in the improvement of the cottage accommodation on those estates, and in the general cultivation of those estates, he was adding a great deal to the prosperity of the county of Northumberland, and to the prosperity of its inhabitants. He alluded to the great interest which his Grace had taken in the formation of this line of railway, and he begged them all to join him in a full and flowing bumper to the long life, health, and prosperity of his Grace the Duke of Northumberland.

This glowing tribute to one of the most generous supporters of the NCR scheme was reinforced by loud cheers from the assembled multitude, but as Earl Percy rose to offer thanks on behalf of the Duke many listeners may have remembered – perhaps with a pang of conscience – the part played by Richard Hodgson in the formation of the Northumberland Central line.

Much good work had also been performed by John Furness Tone and (in a less visible way) by Benjamin Woodman, the Company Secretary; happily, their contribution was openly acknowledged by John Ord who, in a further speech, proposed 'health and happiness to the secretary, engineers, and other officials of the company'. Without a good secretary and good engineers, no railway could be successful, and he had himself witnessed:

> The great zeal which Mr Woodman had brought to bear in the affairs of the company, and also the admirable way in which the engineering business was conducted by Mr Tone, the former engineer, and also by their friend Mr Bruce, and the resident engineer, Mr Holmes, all of whom had brought many good qualities to bear in the construction of the line. (Cheers).

Other speeches were made by the Mayor of Morpeth, by the Reverend G.S. Thompson (Vicar of Acklington) and by Benjamin Woodman. The Reverend Thompson 'looked forward to the period' when the railway would pass through Rothbury 'and onwards towards the sister kingdom of Scotland', while Mr Woodman referred pointedly to the many difficulties that had confronted them since the commencement of the NCR undertaking. They had, he said, met that day to 'celebrate the overcoming of those difficulties' – which had 'not been nominal but *serious*'. However, by acting together in a 'harmonious action' they had brought matters to a satisfactory conclusion; every suggestion that had emanated from the Engineers or himself 'had been met by the Directors in the kindest and best spirit'.

Mr Woodman's short speech made no mention of Richard Hodgson, but his tone was conciliatory, and many listeners felt compelled to applaud his diplomatic remarks. One of the last speakers was George Barclay Bruce, who had replaced Mr Tone as Northumberland Central Engineer. Modestly, he admitted that the difficulties faced by the NCR had been 'financial, rather than engineering', the line itself being a relatively minor engineering project.

In addition to reporting the Opening Day celebrations, the *Newcastle Daily Journal* described the newly-opened railway as follows:

The traveller, as he journeys up the line from Scot's Gap to Rothbury, views on all sides a country of an exceedingly undulating character. Throughout some extent of the dozen miles of rail the gigantic Simonside hills are prominently in view, with their abrupt escarpments and jagged, rugged and heath-cald acclivities, whilst glimpses of the silvery Coquet are here and there to be had, as it winds its way through many a peaceful and picturesque vale. The stations along the route are four in number, namely Scot's Gap, Ewesley, Brinkburn and Rothbury. There is a station at Rothley, but at present it is intended only for the use of Sir Walter Trevelyan's estate.

The steepest gradient on the line is one in sixty; the greatest curve twelve chains in radius. The heaviest cutting is close to Thrum Mill, near to the Rothbury station. The embankment at the viaduct over the Font at Combhill was one of the greatest engineering obstacles the constructors of the line had to contend with, in consequence of the foundation having given way. This embankment was 155 ft long, and the viaduct was the heaviest undertaking on the line so far as masonry was concerned.

The viaduct has twelve arches, each of thirty ft span. The bridge at its greatest height above the bed of the water it crossed was sixty ft. All the stone for the bridge had to be brought a distance of two miles in carts, over very rough roads across a bare moory country.

The highest portion of the line of railway is at a point shortly after leaving the private station of Rothley, a place which is about 694 ft above the level of the sea. Here the passenger has the opportunity of feasting his eyes upon a most beautiful landscape. Beneath him, fed by the Delph burn, lies Rothley lake, situate within Sir Walter Trevelyan's large estate of Wallington. For about three quarters of a mile the watery expanse winds amongst exquisite sylvan scenery – wood, water, and grassy slope commingle in quite 'lake-land' fashion. From this point the line passes on to Ewesley and Nunnykirk, whereabouts may be seen fields wherein the celebrated race horses Beeswing and Tomboy were reared in days gone by.

The line then passes by a heavy gradient to high ground again, through beds of coal, limestone, and shale, the excavation of which was a work of no small difficulty to the constructors, who found here more need for blasting operations than on any other part of the line. Out of this cutting the line is carried on to Forest Burn, where great difficulty was also experienced, in consequence of the embankment giving way upon more than one occasion. Some idea of the great size of this embankment may be formed when it is stated that it consists of about 100,000 cubic yards of earth. It was at this point the construction of the line came to a stand still some time ago, and where the work was again taken up by Mr Bruce, the engineer who succeeded Mr Tone. When the former gentleman and Mr Holmes, the resident engineer, came to examine the line on the resumption of construction, he found it advisable to make the embankment 8 ft 6 in. lower than was at first contemplated. The highest point of this embankment is now 51 ft and its length 600 yards.

Leaving this point the line passes over a dell into which flows two mountain streams – the Cocker and Laudinshaw Burns. After the culvert had been constructed, through which the waters of the united burns flowed, it was found too small. The streams have their sources in the adjacent range, the Simonside hills, and as that Northumbrian watershed oftentimes sends down great floods, it was not long before the necessity arose for constructing a larger artificial watercourse to carry the aggregate waters under the railway embankment.

Brinkburn Station, the next point, is perhaps the most important section of the whole line, in a passenger traffic point of view, as it will accommodate the large district in which lie the two Framlington villages. Here also will, probably, come numerous pic-nic parties in the summer months, for in the valley below is the picturesquely situated Brinkburn Priory, lately restored by the Cadogan family. On the opposite side of the valley to that which the station stands is also to be seen the large works built some years ago for the purpose of smelting iron ore. The works were never in reality in practical working order, for scarcely had smelting commenced before it was discovered that the concern would not pay, for there were no adequate means of conveying the smelted metal from the spot.

As before intimated, the heaviest cutting on the whole line is just before reaching Rothbury Station on the upward journey, where the line is carried through a cutting 280 ft long and 88 ft deep, near to the Thrum Mill. From Rothbury Station a very excellent view of Cragside, the country residence of Sir William Armstrong, is to be had.

It is not necessary here to narrate the untoward circumstances which long delayed the completion of the line. Suffice to say that, when some time ago matters came to a dead-lock, the Duke of Northumberland came to the rescue, and thenceforward all went well with the company. The line of rails is only single throughout the route . . . the line runs through the property of few landlords, the principal being Sir Walter Trevelyan, Mr C.W. Orde of Nunnykirk, and the Duke of Northumberland.

On an optimistic note, the *Newcastle Daily Journal* reporter suggested that the NCR line might one day be extended northwards to Cornhill and south towards Newcastle.

The completed Northumberland Central line was worked by the North British Railway, and the route was, from the earliest days, operated in conjunction with the Scotsgap to Morpeth line. Trains ran through to the Blyth & Tyne station until, in 1872, a physical link was established between the Wansbeck Railway and the NER station at Morpeth.

The Cost of the Line

The railway had cost much more than anyone had expected, and figures released shortly after opening revealed that over £54,000 had been expended on the Northumberland Central line since 1867. Many shareholders blamed Mr Bruce for not keeping construction costs within reasonable limits, and some NCR supporters openly voiced their opinion that Mr Tone should have been allowed to complete the line.

The company's published accounts provide a valuable insight into how the £54,000 had been spent; it is interesting to find, for example, that permanent way materials had absorbed £7,981, while Rothbury station had cost £6,143. The relevant section of the Northumberland Central accounts is shown in the following table, which compares Mr Bruce's estimates with the actual cost of construction.

	Estimates	Actual Costs	Liabilities
Payments to contractors	£26,029	£27,327	£3,834
Sums due to contractor	£4,112	£3,987	£3,834
Permanent way materials	£7,877	£7,981(a)	—
Additional land	£1,270	£1,946	£1,595(b)
Station buildings, sidings & water supply at Rothbury	£5,523	£6,143	£1,752(c)
Law charges	£1,251	£1,895	£1,769
Engineering costs	£2,744	£3,309	£50
Advertising, stationery, etc	£105	£600	£53
Salaries	£500	£542	£192(d)
Interest	—	£647	—
GRAND TOTALS	£49,411	£54,383	£8,247

(a) Includes £117 for materials in stock and available for renewals
(b) Includes rent charges due to Earl Grey and others
(c) Includes Scotsgap turntable and new station at Ewesley
(d) Exclusive of any payments made to NCR Directors

The company's assets totalled £7,447, this sum being computed as follows:

Balance in hand £41
Arrears of call on share capital £247
Balance to be received from Duke of Northumberland under
certificates for additional borrowing powers £2,565
Preference shares under ditto available for issue £3,500
Balance of available loan powers £1,094

The North British Takeover

The Northumberland Central company struggled on for a few months as an independent company, but the 13 mile Rothbury branch was a great disappointment to its promoters, and although the line was clearly of some benefit to the local community, the NCR supporters soon lost interest in their scheme. Company meetings were frequently the scene of bitter recriminations, the usual pattern being for Richard Hodgson (no longer on the Board but still a force to be reckoned with in NCR affairs) to complain loudly about what he saw as gross mismanagement.

There had, in the meantime, been several organisational changes. Earl Grey, for instance had left the Board, his position as Chairman being filled by Sir Walter Calverley Trevelyan. Although the Duke of Northumberland was not a Director, he had retained a large financial stake in the NCR – his dealings with the Northumberland Central being handled by his agent, Mr Snowball. Sir John Swinburne, John Bolam, and George Culley had retired from the Board, the vacant places being taken by William Forster (Junior) of Rothbury, Thomas Gow of Cambo, John Marshall of Chatton Park, John Dodd Wealleans of Flotterton and Henry Thomas Morton of Fence Houses, Durham.

The new Board struggled with a variety of problems, and although lack of money was the overriding difficulty, the personal antipathy between Richard Hodgson and his rivals on the Board can have done little to ease the situation. Mr Hodgson (who was now calling himself Richard Hodgson-Huntley) had apparently developed a particular aversion towards Mr Snowball, and the protagonists were not afraid to attack each other publicly in the pages of the local press.

The general public inevitably suspected a split between the Duke of Northumberland and Mr Hodgson, and in June 1871 Mr Hodgson – perhaps feeling that he had gone too far in his criticisms of the Duke and his agent – wrote a somewhat grudging letter of apology to *The Railway Times*. Denying that he had ever spoken 'in disparaging terms' of the Duke's conduct, he reminded readers that his grace had shown great 'liberality in subscribing . . . £14,000 of the company's ordinary shares'. Having praised the Duke for saving the scheme in this way, Mr Hodgson returned to the attack over the dismissal of Mr Tone.

The abrupt dismissal of John Furness Tone was evidently a particular source of bitterness, and when, on 17th June, 1871, *The Railway Times* reported a recently-held Northumberland Central meeting, much column space was allocated to Mr Hodgson's long-standing complaints. Some of the more salient points are worth quoting insofar as they underline the gulf that had appeared between Mr Hodgson and his former co-Directors:

> Mr Huntley thought it was a great pity that they got into such a hobble by wasting their capital, and he was free to state that it had been caused mainly by the dismissal of their first engineer. Everything had gone wrong since Mr Tone left the works . . . if Mr Tone had been allowed to continue his labours to the end he would, by constant supervision and a thorough knowledge of the works he was undertaking, in all their details, have executed them very much more cheaply than had been the case since he left. It was quite clear there was good ground for that belief because when Mr Tone presented his estimate to the Directors in 1868 for which he would undertake to complete the line, the sum of money did not even reach £40,000.

Mr Hodgson pointed out that the actual cost of completing the line 'was not far short of £55,000', and although he did not blame the new Engineer, he thought it had been 'against wisdom' for the company to change Engineers when things had been going so well.

Referring to an arrangement made between George Barclay Bruce and the Duke of Northumberland whereby the new Engineer would report directly to the Duke, Mr Hodgson continued as follows:

> It was understood . . . that another engineer should report to the Duke of Northumberland, and no doubt he did report faithfully to the best of the lights he could obtain; but it was very evident that nobody but the engineer who had carried the work on from the commencement could either give a fair estimate as to costs, or execute the work with the same economy. When Mr Bruce thus came upon the field, the Directors of the company, very unwisely indeed, adopted him as engineer of the line instead of coadjutor to Mr Tone, who had up to that time been going on at a saving on the schedule prices of the contractors.
>
> No sooner did the new system come in than excesses appeared in every item of the estimates. The amount crept up from £44,000 to £49,000, yet in spite of proposed schemes of reductions and promises not to charge engineering fees if the estimate was exceeded, the actual cost, according to Mr Bruce's own showing, was

not now far short of £55,000; and even this would have been increased by £1,200 or £1,500 if the company had had the honesty to publish the interest on debentures on what they considered a fair statement of accounts.

In most of his reports Mr Bruce had addressed himself to Mr Snowball, the Duke's agent, as though that gentleman had been the Board of Directors and, to say the least of it, this was neither satisfactory nor fair to the company. Now, his firm conviction was, that if Mr Tone had remained in the service of the company up to the present time the line would have been completed at an earlier period, and at £10,000 less cost. He said this more in justification of Mr Tone, and in condemnation of the manner in which he was dismissed, than as any kind of censure upon Mr Bruce; because he was quite aware that it was impossible for any new engineer, unacquainted with details, to carry out the scheme so successfully as the original undertaker. A more short-sighted act was never performed than the dismissal of Mr Tone, for although they might have saved a little in engineer's salary, they had incurred the present extraordinary expenditure in consequence.

Continuing his unabated tirade against all aspects of Northumberland Central policy, Mr Hodgson next attacked the unsatisfactory operating agreement with the North British Railway; he saw no quick or easy solutions to any of these problems, though they should (he thought) 'try to get better traffic, better terms for working, and, as soon as some fairly reasonable price for was offered for the line, then they must, for goodness sake, accept it'.

The next speaker was Mr Bruce, who claimed that the speech just made by Mr Hodgson-Huntley 'was made not so much to enlighten the shareholders as it was intended as an attack upon himself'. It would, he said, have been much better if Mr Hodgson had voiced his opinions *before* the Directors sanctioned a change of Engineers, but before this theme could be developed Mr Hodgson interrupted to say that he was abroad at the time. Ignoring this very valid point, Mr Bruce added that the criticism was 'altogether very unfair'; it was all very well to say that the cost had been excessive, 'but that was a style of reasoning which would not for a moment bear the light'. He strongly denied that Mr Tone's estimate had ever been as low as £40,000, and to prove the point he held up a document in which his predecessor had clearly stipulated a figure of £44,000. The latter sum, suggested Mr Bruce, was very close to his own estimate of £47,000, but as liabilities of £2,411 had been due before he replaced Mr Tone, the estimate had been increased accordingly. On top of this continued the Engineer, it had been found necessary to add a turntable at Scotsgap, and there were numerous other alterations that had not been anticipated when he agreed to work for the NCR. It was obvious, therefore, that by 'deducting these matters, law charges and other things from the amount of excess', the difference between Mr Tone's estimate and his own was 'considerably short of £2,000'. Indeed, he added, much of the £2,000 difference had been caused by 'the slipping away of the banks':

> He had only to say further that he had not solicited the duty; that it was at the pressing request of the Directors that he had consented to act both for the Duke and themselves; and that, owing to the work having gone on so slowly for want of funds, he had actually spent in the interests of the company every farthing he had ever received from it, and had not one fraction of a farthing for himself. Although he had never expected much from the undertaking, he must say that he had not

been slow to look after the interests of the shareholders, and that he had taken £500 worth of debentures for the purpose of helping them on. He had, of course written his reports to Mr Snowball, and, as he represented the Duke of Northumberland in the matter, it could not be denied that he was right, but . . . a copy of every such communication was also sent for the inspection of the Directors of the company.

In reply, Mr Hodgson-Huntley denied that his attack had been directed against Mr Bruce on a personal level; his criticisms were against the policy of changing Engineers when everything had been proceeding satisfactorily under Mr Tone. It appears, however, that Mr Hodgson could not resist the temptation to attack the hapless Mr Bruce on the matter of gradients, which 'he understood had been changed from 1 in 65 to 1 in 62 without any authority, and then re-altered at the expense of the company'. Incensed at this trivial criticism, Mr Bruce exclaimed 'that is not true', and Mr Hodgson responded as follows:

> I am only going upon the information of others, and they tell me the slopes are not finished in a manner conducive to the economical working of the line in the future. The result of all this is that we are heavily indebted, and liable to very serious consequences.

Unable to let this criticism of his work pass unanswered, Mr Bruce explained that the gradients had been altered by a minimal amount 'with the express view and actual effect' of saving money. If he had not done so, the expense would have been much greater, and he did not see how the company could have afforded any additional cost.

The Chairman, Sir Walter Trevelyan, tried to end the row by saying that Mr Hodgson-Huntley did not wish to say anything offensive, while the explanation of Mr Bruce was entirely satisfactory. He did not wish to see the scheme collapse, and in fact he had little doubt that the railway's traffic returns would soon allow them to pay off their debts. Trying to put matters into an optimistic light, he suggested that the traffic returns were satisfactory and would probably increase'. Already, he added, 'many applications had been made for building sites about Rothbury', and 'as the villages extended, and the number of buildings increased, so would the traffic of the line be augmented, and hence . . . their undertaking would ultimately prove very satisfactory both to shareholders and the residents in the neighbourhood'.

John Ord proposed that a committee of shareholders and Directors could be appointed 'to confer with the neighbouring companies as to the working of the line', but this course of action found little favour; he also asked if the Duke of Northumberland might be persuaded to advance 'a further sum of £5,000' – though it seemed unlikely that the Duke would wish to commit himself in this way. In the end, the assembled proprietors decided that they would leave things in the hands of the Directors, on the assumption that the Board would 'know best how to avert the critical position of the company'.

Sadly, the Northumberland Central Directors did not know how to extricate themselves from the morass into which they had so rapidly descended, and as 1871 drew to a close the idea of a sale to one or other of the main line companies became increasingly attractive. The Directors were, after all, merely local gentlemen who had wished to bring rail communication to their own farms and villages, and having built the railway their primary object had been achieved.

The thought of a sale carried no stigma of failure, and indeed, by divesting themselves of the railway the Directors would doubtless have felt that a heavy load had been lifted from their shoulders. One small question in the event of a sale, was whether the Northumberland Central should be sold to the North British or the North Eastern companies. In reality, the only realistic course of action would be sale to the NBR, which had worked the line from its inception. The Northumberland Central connected with the North British at Scotsgap, and although the North Eastern was still interested in extending its influence in the area, the Rothbury branch was hardly a suitable candidate for NER control; if the link to Cornhill had been built the situation would clearly have been more flexible, but under the circumstances there was little incentive for the NER to acquire a short branch line with no physical connections to its own system.

Events were now leading inexorably towards an amalgamation with the North British Railway, and in July 1872 the Northumberland Central Railway was absorbed by its mighty neighbour. Northumberland Central shareholders were suitably compensated, the holders of NCR ordinary stock receiving a preferential dividend of 1 per cent from 1st February 1877, while NCR preference stock was guaranteed at 5 per cent for an initial period of five years. From 1st February, 1878 the ordinary shareholders were promised an increased dividend (subject to the performance of North British ordinary stock), and NCR preference shareholders were to receive a 4 per cent dividend after the first five year period. At the same time, the North British Railway paid £9,000 to discharge all NCR liabilities, while the mortgage debt of £21,706 was converted into North British 4 per cent debenture stock in 1877.

Henceforth, the Rothbury branch would become a mere appendage of the NBR – though, as we shall see, the demise of the Northumberland Central company did not extinguish the long-standing plans for extension beyond Rothbury. There were, indeed, rumours to the effect that having gained control of the NCR the North British would seek control of the Blyth & Tyne Railway between Morpeth and Newcastle. Acquisition of the Blyth & Tyne would have given the NBR an independent route to Newcastle via Reedsmouth and Scotsgap, but the thought of Scottish trains reaching Tyneside in this way so alarmed the North Eastern Directors that, in 1874, the NER itself secured control of the Blyth & Tyne Railway. The route from Morpeth to Tyneside thereby passed into 'enemy' hands and, as a corollary of this development, the eastern section of the Wansbeck Railway lost its chance to become part of a North British through route.

There remained a possibility that independent access to the Newcastle area might be achieved by means of the so-called 'South Northumberland' route via Scotsgap; such a line had been proposed in the 1860s as a natural southern extension of the Northumberland Central, but sadly, the scheme had been a total failure.

In the meantime, the North British management had initiated several improvements on the former Northumberland Central line, one of the first of

these changes being at Longwitton, where the private station known as
'Rothley' was brought into use as a public stopping place. At Rothbury, the
NCR terminus was substantially improved while, in the next few years,
there would be considerable new development in terms of new sidings to
serve Ewesley Quarry, Whitehouse limeworks and other lineside industries – all of which were able to benefit from the provision of rail transport
facilities in the Rothbury area.

Ex-NER 'J21' class 0–6–0 No. 65035 enters Morpeth station with a Rothbury freight
working in September 1952. The Wansbeck route was, at this point, parallel to the
East Coast main line.   *J.W. Armstrong*

Gradient profile of the Rothbury branch from Scotsgap Junction.

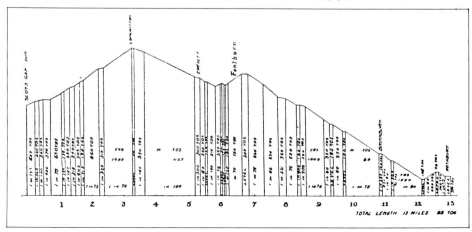

Rothbury station in the 1950s, with class 'J25' 0−6−0 No. 65727 standing beside the water tank. Note the grounded coach body and also the ornate platform canopy valance.

E.E. Smith

Ivatt 2−6−0 No. 46474 on a local pick-up goods service at Longwitton.

W.S. Sellar

Class 'J1' No. 65103 with a full head of steam standing in the platform at Scotsgap (c.1950) with a local pick-up goods.

E.E. Smith

LNER 0–4–4 tank No. 1745 on the two-coach local service to Rothbury, seen here at Scotsgap.

E.E. Smith, courtesy Neville Stead

Chapter Three

A Northumbrian Branch Line (1880–1947)

The Northumberland Central Railway Company may have ceased to exist as a separate entity in 1872, but there were still lingering hopes that the line between Scotsgap Junction and Rothbury might be utilised as part of a cross country route linking Newcastle and Scotland. These hopes came very close to reality in the early 1880s when, having considered the transport interests of small towns and villages such as Wooler, Glanton and Wooperton, a group of local entrepreneurs decided to proceed with a scheme for connecting lines between Newcastle and Wooperton.

Plans for the 'Central Northumberland Railway' were deposited in 1881. The scheme provided for two geographically separate lines, one of which would run from Newcastle to Scotsgap via Ponteland and Belsay, while the other would continue the Rothbury branch northwards from Rothbury to Wooler via Thropton, Alnham and Wooperton. The Central Northumberland proposals were tacitly supported by the North British Railway, but although (on the surface) the scheme seemed nothing more than an innocuous plan to bring rail transport to a remote rural area, the North Eastern Railway objected to the presence of the NBR at Newcastle. In the interim, the English-based North Eastern company had itself formulated a rival scheme for construction of a circuitous line from Alnwick to Coldstream via Glanton, Wooperton and Akeld.

There were thus, by 1881, plans for two lines in the area north of Rothbury – one of which would connect with the Rothbury branch whereas the other (NER) line would form part of a 'loop' between Alnmouth, Alnwick, Coldstream and Tweedmouth. Meanwhile, Cornelius and George Lundie – two London-based engineers – had entered the fray with proposals for a 3 ft narrow gauge line from Rothbury to Kelso. Pointing out that a narrow gauge line would be much cheaper than a comparable standard gauge railway, the engineers estimated that their 3 ft gauge 'Rothbury, Wooler & Kelso Railway' could be built at a cost of £3,713 per mile, the total cost (including land) being £4,000 per mile. They anticipated that local landowners would be prepared 'to deal with the railway company on very liberal terms', while further assistance might be rendered by Parliament.

The arguments in favour of a 3 ft gauge line from Rothbury to Kelso were set out in a pamphlet published in July 1881. This purported to show that a railway could be made 'suited to the requirements of Central Northumberland and the north-eastern corner of Roxburghshire at a cost of less than £5,000 per mile, with the prospect of a fair return of profit on the outlay'. The line proposed was to run via 'Thropton, Lorbottle, Whittingham, Glanton, Wooperton, Lilburn, Middleton, Wooler, Akeld, Kirk Newton, Kilham, Paston, Yetholm, Primside, Morebattle and Kalemouth' beyond which the route would converge with the NBR near Kelso. The distance from Rothbury to Kelso would be about 50 miles, including three miles of mixed gauge line between Heiton Sidings and Kelso NBR station. The line would not form part of a through route, but as the promoters pointed out, neither would the rival North Eastern scheme:

For obvious reasons, the proposed railway would not form part of a through route competing for traffic with the great lines of communication from North to South, but it is plain that the line from Rothbury to Cornhill and Alnwick, which is understood to have been lately proposed by the North Eastern Railway Company, neither would, nor could, be used for such a purpose.

Neither could the suggested narrow gauge line be extended southwards to Newcastle, because the 3 ft gauge 'would not be suitable' for the 'necessities of the southern portion of Northumberland; this part of the Newcastle to Kelso route should (argued the pro-narrow gauge pamphleteers) 'be taken up by the North British Railway Company, or, at all events, under their auspices, seeing that all the railways at Scotsgap belong to them'. The pamphlet went on to suggest that a 50 mile narrow gauge line could be built for around £220,117, including £29,604 for earthworks, £70,875 for permanent way, and £32,190 for 'locomotive engines, carriages and wagons of various sorts'.

It is unclear if these narrow gauge proposals were ever intended to be taken seriously – the scheme may well have been merely an academic exercise designed to prove that the 3 ft gauge could be adapted for use on the British mainland (3 ft gauge lines were then enjoying unexpected popularity in Ireland). Alternatively, George and Cornelius Lundie may have hoped that by publishing their plans at a time when the NBR and NER proposals were under consideration they would be able to influence public opinion in favour of the North British scheme – their 1881 pamphlet was certainly biased in favour of the NBR. If this was indeed the case the ploy was a total failure, and in 1882 Parliament finally decided in favour of the North Eastern line from Alnwick to Coldstream. This line – sometimes referred to as the Cornhill Branch – was finally completed in 1887, by which time the narrow gauge project had been consigned to oblivion.

As far as the Rothbury branch was concerned, the opening of the Cornhill line heralded the ultimate victory of the North Eastern Railway in its desire to stop further NBR expansion in central Northumberland. The North Eastern had effectively blocked the northwards path to Scotland, and with NER trains running through Glanton, Wooperton, Ilderton and Wooler, it was clear that the Rothbury branch would never be able to reach its ultimate Scottish goal.

Having failed to become part of a through route to Scotland via Coldstream, the Scotsgap to Rothbury line settled down to a peaceful existence as a very rural branch line, with a meagre train service on the 24¼ mile route between Morpeth, Scotsgap and Rothbury. Trains connected with the North Eastern system at Morpeth, but there was little attempt to provide a comparable connection to and from the North British network via Reedsmouth Junction. There were, it is true, connecting services between Scotsgap and the Border Union line, but potential through travellers were faced with long and boring waits at Scotsgap, Reedsmouth or Riccarton junctions, and only the most hardened travellers would have willingly chosen to reach Glasgow or Edinburgh via the NBR Border Counties and Waverley routes.

Rail facilities were nevertheless instrumental in placing Rothbury and the surrounding area on the Victorian tourist's map, and by the turn-of-the-century the town had emerged as a minor golfing and fishing resort. This development was obviously welcomed by the North British Railway which (like all Scottish lines) did much to persuade golfers and other upper middle class holiday makers to spend long or short holidays in resorts served by the North British system.

Some Effects of the Railway

Rothbury was changed in many ways by the coming of the railway – the town was, for example, substantially rebuilt in the years following 1870, many new houses and public buildings being erected in the final quarter of the 19th century. Edwardian editions of *Kelly's Directory of Northumberland* provide an interesting glimpse of Rothbury at this time, and the following extract underlines the extent to which the town had developed as a tourist resort by 1912:

ROTHBURY, anciently 'Roberie' and 'Routhbyrig', is a township, parish and head of a union and county court district, situated within a bend of the River Coquet, here crossed by a substantial stone bridge of four arches, and is the terminus of a branch from Scot's Gap junction on the North British Railway, 306 miles from London, 30 north-west from Newcastle, 15 north-south-west from Morpeth, 12 south-west from Alnwick, 31 north-by-east from Hexham, 14 from Cheviot and 16 miles from the sea, in the Hexham division of the county, west division of Coquetdale ward, Coquetdale West petty sessional division, and in the rural deanery of Rothbury, archdeanery of Lindisfarne and diocese of Newcastle. The parish is about 32 miles in circumference, and considerable improvements were made within it in 1865–70.

The town, which is governed by an Urban District Council of nine members, formed under the provisions of the Local Government Act 1894 (56 & 57 Vic cap 73) is much resorted to by visitors in the summer season on account of its salubrious air, magnificent scenery and the excellent trout fishing in the Coquet; it is well sheltered from the north and east winds by a lofty ridge of steep and rugged rocks, and on the south side rise the sharp jagged edges of Simonside, some 1,500 ft above the sea, from the summit of which, on a clear day, can be seen the whole coast of Northumberland from Berwick-on-Tweed to the Tyne, a distance of about 60 miles.

The town is lighted by gas by the Rothbury Gas Co. and supplied with excellent water from springs at Swanwell and Simonside . . . The Mechanics' Institute, established in 1850, is supplied with newspapers and has a good library containing about 2,500 volumes, and a billiard room. A Jubilee Hall, in conjunction with the Mechanics' Institute, was erected by subscription in 1887, at a cost of about £760, and again enlarged in 1897, when a dining hall and committee rooms were added at a further cost of £800; the hall is used for lectures, concerts and entertainments, and will hold 300 persons. Steeplchases are held here annually. Here is a 9-hole golf course. Fairs are held here on the Friday in the Easter week, Whit-Monday, October 2nd and November 1st. Markets for the sale of livestock are held every alternate Monday, and special sales for store sheep every fortnight from July till November by Messrs Donkin & Son.

The principal hotels are the County, Queen's Head and Station; the Station Hotel, close by the North British Railway terminus, contains 30 rooms and a posting yard. The County Hotel stands in beautifully laid-out grounds by the River Coquet, and contains upwards of 50 rooms . . . The area of the township and Urban

District is 945 acres of land and 25 of water; rateable value, £6,916; the population in 1911 was 1,147, including 4 officers and 44 inmates in the Union Workhouse, and of the ecclesiastical parish, 2,337.

A further view of Edwardian Rothbury comes from the pen of R. Lendrem-Ainslie. Writing in the January 1917 *Railway Magazine*, he echoed *Kelly's Directory* in his description of a small, but prosperous golfing and fishing resort:

> Of the picturesque little town of Rothbury it may be said that in the Newcastle and Northumberland districts it has been somewhat generally recognised as a health resort for nearly half a century, while as a rural retreat the wonder and charm of its wild beauties has long been known and appreciated ... To the disciples of Isaac Walton the district is indeed an angler's paradise. The Duke of Northumberland has recently leased the whole of his waters on the River Coquet, famous for its yellow trout, bull trout and salmon, to the Coquet Committee of the Northumberbrian Anglers' Federation, and permits to anglers are issued for short or long periods at very cheap rates.
>
> There is also an excellent 9-hole golf course, which is situated in high ground to the south of the town. This course is remarkable in many ways. The natural undulations of the grass land and the two picturesque ravines which it crosses have rendered artificial bunkers unnecessary, while considerable variety has been shown in the situation of the various greens, and in the arranging of the course every opportunity has been taken to involve the several hazards which are offered by the natural features. The site of the course is one of exceptional beauty and commands views of some of the most impressive and characteristic scenery in the Rothbury district.

Although the outbreak of World War I had prevented the North British Railway from 'extensively advertising the well-merited claims of Rothbury as a summer health and visitor resort', Mr Lendrom-Ainslie hoped that, after the war, 'the restricted train service' that had hitherto been provided would be improved.

Branch Passenger Services

In the event, the meagre train services between Rothbury and Morpeth were never increased; after all, the branch ran through a remote and inhospitable area, and tourism notwithstanding, passenger traffic was never heavy. There were, for many years, just three trains each way between Morpeth and Rothbury, with an extra working on Wednesdays and Saturdays only.

In 1911, the first up service left Rothbury at 7.50 am, and, pursuing its leisurely way across the Northumbrian moors, this early morning working reached Scotsgap at 8.22 am. Having made a connection with the 7.43 am local service from Reedsmouth, the branch train resumed its journey at 8.24 am, and at 8.48 it arrived at the junction. The corresponding down working left Morpeth at 9.25 am and arrived back at Rothbury by 10.53 am, prior to forming the 11.28 up service to Morpeth; the latter reached its destination at 12.32 pm and there was, thereafter, a two hour gap before the branch train set off back to Rothbury at 2.25 pm. The third and last return trip to Morpeth was made at 4.30 pm, and having reached the junction at

MORPETH BRANCH.—North British.

Miles	Up.	Mls		Week Days. mrn	mrn	aft
	Reedsmouth...dep.			7 47	11 5	4 30
3¾	Woodburn			7 56	1114	4 39
10¼	Knowesgate			8 11	1129	4 54
—		Mls	Rothbury..dep.	7 50	1128	4 30
—		2¼	Brinkburn	7 56	1134	4 36
—		6¼	Fontburn	8 7	1145	4 47
—		7¾	Ewesley	8 11	1150	4 53
—		9¾	Longwitton	8 17	1156	4 59
—		13	Scotsgap*..arr.	8 24	12 1	5 6
14	Scotsgap*			8 26	12 3	5 9
16	Middleton			8 31	12 8	5 15
17¼	Angerton			8 35	1213	5 20
19¾	Meldon........[691			8 44	1222	5 29
25	Morpeth 690, arr			8 55	1232	5 39

Miles	Down.	Week Days. mrn	aft	aft
	Morpeth.......dep.	9 25	2 25	6c20
5¼	Meldon	9 38	2 38	6 33
7¼	Angerton	9 44	2 44	6 39
9	Middleton	9 49	2 49	6 44
11	Scotsgap*	9 55	2 55	6 50
—	Scotsgap.....dep.	9 57	2 57	6 52
14¼	Longwitton	10 6	3 6	7 1
16¼	Ewesley	1012	3 12	7 7
17¼	Fontburn	1016	3 16	7 11
21¾	Brinkburn	1028	3 28	7 23
24	Rothbury....arr.	1035	3 35	7 30
14¾	Knowesgate	1018	3 11	7 6
21¼	Woodburn	1032	3 25	7 20
25	Reedsmouth (above)	1040	3 33	7 28

NOTES.

c Waits till 7 aft. for N.E. connections.

* Station for Cambo.

Bradshaw's Timetable for April 1910.

MORPETH BRANCH.—North British.

Miles	Up.	Mls		Week Days only. mrn (Through Carriage to Newcastle, see page 735.)	mrn	aft (From Bellingham at 4 5 aft., see page 809.)	aft (Tuesdays only.)
	Reedsmouth...dep.			8 0	1120	4 15	6 5
3¾	Woodburn			8 10	1129	4 24	6 14
10¼	Knowesgate §			8 26	1144	4 39	6 29
14	Scotsgap‡......arr.			8 35	1153	4 48	6 38
—		Mls	Rothbury..dep.	8 9	1130	4 29	
—		2¼	Brinkburn	8 14	1135	4 34	
—		6¼	Fontburn Halt	8 26	1147	4 46	
—		7¾	Ewesley	8 30	1151	4 50	
—		9¾	Longwitton	8 36	1157	4 56	
—		13	Scotsgap‡..arr.	8 42	12 3	5 2	
—	Scotsgap.......dep.			8 44	12 5	5 4	
16	Middleton			8 49	1210	5 9	
17¼	Angerton			8 53	1214	5 13	
19¾	Meldon...[735,745			8 59	1220	5 19	
25	Morpeth 734, arr.			9 9	1230	5 29	

Miles	Down.	Week Days only. mrn	aft (To Bellingham (arr. 3 41 aft.), see page 809.)	aft (Tuesdays only.)	aft (Through Carriage from Newcastle, see page 734.)	aft (Tuesdays only.)
	Morpeth........dep.	9 45	2 15		5 55	
5¼	Meldon	9 58	2 28		6 8	
7¼	Angerton	10 4	2 34		6 14	
9	Middleton	10 9	2 39		6 19	
11	Scotsgap‡......arr.	1015	2 45		6 25	
—	Scotsgap......dep.	1017	2 47		6 27	
14¼	Longwitton	1026	2 56		6 36	
16¼	Ewesley	1031	3 1		6 42	
17¼	Fontburn Halt	1035	3 5		6 46	
21¼	Brinkburn	1045	3 15		6 56	
24	Rothbury.....arr.	1051	3 21		7 2	
—	Scotsgap........dep.	1022	2 54	5 8	6H32	6 45
14¾	Knowesgate §	1033	3 5	5 19	6H43	6 56
21¼	Woodburn	1047	3 19	5 33	6H57	7 10
25	Reedsmouth 809 arr.	1055	3 27	5 41	7H5	7 18

H Except Tuesdays. ‡ Station for Cambo (1 mile). § Station for Kirkwhelpington (1 mile).

Bradshaw's Timetable for June 1922.

MORPETH, SCOTSGAP, REEDSMOUTH, and ROTHBURY

Miles	Down	Week Days mrn	aft J	aft S	aft T	aft J	aft E	aft S	Sun mrn	Sun aft
	Morpeth........dep.	10 1	215	F	..	5 45	9 50	9 50	1027	9 45
5¼	Meldon	1013	228	..	..	5 58	10 3	10 3	1039	9 57
7¼	Angerton	1019	234	..	..	6 4	10 9	10 9	1045	10 3
9	Middleton North	1023	239	..	..	6 9	..	1014	..	..
11	Scotsgap B	1029	245	..	..	6 15	1018	1020	1054	1012
—	Scotsgap......dep.	1034	..	254	5 1	6A22	..	..	..	..
14½	Knowesgate A	1043	..	3 5	511	6A33	..	..	..	..
21¼	Woodburn (above)	1056	..	319	525	6A47	..	..	..	..
25	Reedsmouth..arr.	11 3	..	327	533	6A55	..	..	..	..
14½	Longwitton	1040	255	..	..	6 26	..	1030	..	..
16½	Ewesley	1045	3 0	..	..	6 32	1032	1036	11 8	1026
17½	Fontburn Halt	1049	3 4	..	..	6 36	1036	1040	..	..
21½	Brinkburn	1058	313	..	..	6F45	..	1049	..	..
24	Rothbury.......arr.	11 4	319	..	..	6 51	1049	1055	1123	1041

Miles	Up	Mls		Week Days mn D	mrn S	mrn	aft H	aft	aft T	aft E	aft S	Sun mrn	Sun aft
	Rothbury.......dep.			8 5	..	1130	..	425	..	722	828	1136	835
2¼	Brinkburn			810	..	1135	..	430	..	D	833	..	..
6¼	Fontburn Halt			821	..	1146	..	441	..	..	844	..	..
7¾	Ewesley			824	..	1149	..	444	..	..	847	1151	850
9¾	Longwitton			830	..	1155	..	450	..	..	853	..	..
—		Mls	Reedsmouth dep.	753	1120	..	415	..	6 0	..	D	..	..
—		3¾	Woodburn	8 4	1129	..	424	..	6 9	..	..	..	..
—		10¼	Knowesgate A	820	1144	..	439	..	624	..	..	..	..
—		14	Scotsgap B arr.	829	1153	..	448	..	633	..	..	..	..
13	Scotsgap B			839	..	12 2	..	457	..	745	9 0	12 2	9 1
15	Middleton North			844	..	12 6	..	5 1	..	750	9 5		9 6
16½	Angerton			849	..	1210	..	5 5	..	..	9 9	12 9	911
18¼	Meldon [833, 966			856	..	1215	..	510	..	..	914	1214	916
24	Morpeth 830, arr.			9 8	..	1225	..	520	..	8 5	924	1224	926

A Sta for Kirkwhelpington (1 mle) Ⱥ 20 mins later Tues B Sta for Cambo (1 mle) D Thro Carrs, Rothbury to Newcastle, page 833. E Except Sats F To Bellingham, arr 3 41 aft, above ғ Stops to set down H From Bellingham dep 4 5 aft, above J Thro' Carrs., Newcastle to Rothbury, page 831 S Sats. only T Tues. only

Bradshaw's Timetable for July 1938.

Tables 164 & 164a MORPETH, SCOTSGAP, and REEDSMOUTH, and ROTHBURY

Miles		Week Days only mrn		aft S		aft		
	157 NEWCASTLE ... dep	9 35	..	1A12	..	5 7	..	..
—	Morpeth .... dep	10 8	..	2 15	..	5 45	..	..
5½	Meldon	10 20	...	2 28	..	5 58	..	..
7¾	Angerton	10 27	..	2 34	..	6 4	..	..
9¾	Middleton North	10 32	..	2 39	..	6 9	..	..
11½	Scotsgap D	10 38	..	2 45	..	6 15	..	..
—	Scotsgap .... dep	10 44	..	..	..	6 22	..	..
15	Knowesgate	10 53	..	..	..	6 33	..	..
21½	Woodburn	11 6	..	..	..	6 47	..	..
25½	Reedsmouth.... arr	11 13	..	..	..	6 55	..	..
14½	Longwitton	10 50	..	2 55	..	6 26	..	..
16½	Ewesley	10 55	..	3 0	..	6 33	..	..
17½	Fontburn Halt	11 0	..	3 4	..	6 38	..	..
22	Brinkburn	11 10	..	3 13	..	6F47	..	..
24¼	Rothbury......... arr	11 16	..	3 19	..	6 53	..	..

Miles		Mls		Week Days only mrn		mrn S		aft				
	Rothbury......... dep			7 50	..	1130	..	4 25	..	..	..	..
2¼	Brinkburn			7 55	..	1135	..	4 30	..	..	..	..
6½	Fontburn Halt			8 6	..	1146	..	4 41	..	..	..	..
7¾	Ewesley			8 9	..	1149	..	4 44	..	..	..	..
9½	Longwitton			8 15	..	1155	..	4 50	..	..	..	..
—		Mls	Reedsmouth.. dep	7 40	..	..	..	4 15	..	..	..	..
—		3¾	Woodburn	7 51	..	..	..	4 24	..	..	..	..
—		10¼	Knowesgate	8 7	..	..	..	4 39	..	..	..	..
—		14	Scotsgap D... arr	8 16	..	..	..	4 48	..	..	..	..
13	Scotsgap D			8 24	..	12 2	..	4 57	..	..	..	..
15	Middleton North			8 29	..	12 6	..	5 1	..	..	..	..
16½	Angerton			8 34	..	1210	..	5 5	..	..	..	..
18¾	Meldon			8 41	..	1215	..	5 10	..	..	..	..
24¼	Morpeth .... arr			8 53	..	1225	..	5 20	..	..	..	..
40¼	157 NEWCASTLE ... arr			9 30	..	2 1	..	6 5	..	..	..	..

A Manors North, Newcastle. D Station for Cambo (1 mile). ғ Calls to set down only S Saturdays only.

Bradshaw's Timetable for February 1942.

5.39, the branch train left Morpeth at 6.20. Finally, at 7.30 pm, the train pulled in to Rothbury, and after running-round, the locomotive ran light to the nearby engine shed for routine servicing.

Mails were conveyed by the three up trains and by the afternoon and evening down workings; there was a letter box at the station, and this was cleared at 10.25 am, 3.20 and 5.30 pm.

Freight Traffic

Freight traffic carried on the Rothbury branch was mainly agricultural, with a particular emphasis on livestock and wool. Coal mining and quarrying were also important at various times, although most of the local mines and quarries were small-scale ventures employing no more than a handful of miners or quarrymen. Mining was, moreover a transcient activity, and many local mines or quarries lasted for only a few years; the Brinkburn Coal Company, for instance, had closed its small pit near Brinkburn station by 1925. Lord Armstrong, the arms manufacturer, employed several quarrymen in the Rothbury area, though it is believed that much of the local stone was used on Armstrong's own estate at 'Cragside'. Some coal, limestone and whinstone was nevertheless exported by rail, not only from Rothbury but also from Longwitton and the intermediate stations en route to Scotsgap Junction.

Rothbury and the intermediate stations were equipped with sidings and loading banks for the loading and unloading of goods and mineral traffic, but the facilities provided varied considerably – some stations having full goods-handling facilities while others had only rudimentary provision for goods traffic. Large, overall goods sheds were not a feature of the former Northumberland Central line, although Rothbury itself boasted a small goods warehouse. Privately-owned mineral lines were found at Longwitton, Fontburn and near Rothbury, and these dealt with coal, limestone and whinstone traffic.

Successive editions of *The Railway Clearing House Handbook of Stations* are a useful source of information in relation to goods-handling facilities, particularly where private sidings were concerned. As mentioned above, extractive industries such as coal mining were, by their very nature, impermanent, and it follows that sidings laid to serve particular collieries often had very short lives.

The following table, compiled with reference to the *Railway Clearing House Handbook*, shows the sidings en route to Rothbury in the 1920s and early 1930s, together with the other goods facilities at each station. Although a key is given at the end of the table, it may be worth adding that the letter 'L' indicates that the stations concerned had cattle docks, while the presence of 'H' or 'C' in the table shows that loading docks were available for the shipment of horses or motor vehicles. The latter were invariably loaded via end-loading bays, 'motor car vans' having end doors through which road vehicles could be driven under their own power. Fixed hand cranes were provided only at 'large' stations such as Rothbury, but rail-mounted cranes could easily be sent to wayside stations if loads of timber or other heavy consignments were sent by rail.

The situation regarding 'sidings' is slightly confusing in that the names conferred on certain sidings did not always reflect their geographical location – Ewesley Siding, for instance, was actually at Fontburn. The table does, however, underline the relative importance of private siding traffic, and although stations such as Ewesley and Brinkburn did not in themselves contribute much traffic, the neighbouring goods lines contributed coal or mineral traffic that would otherwise have been loaded in the goods yard. (See Chapter Four for further details of some of these obscure lines). For completeness, the table includes the Wansbeck Valley stations at Meldon, Middleton and Angerton, which were served by Rothbury branch freights on their way to and from Morpeth.

Table 1

GOODS & PASSENGER ACCOMMODATION ON THE ROTHBURY LINE

Station	m.	ch.	Facilities	Crane	Sidings
Meldon	05	31	G P F L H C	—	
Angerton	07	53	G P F L H C	—	
Middleton	09	13	G P L H	—	
Scotsgap	11	11	G P F L H C	2 tons	
Long Witton	14	35	G P F L H C	—	{*Longwitton Colliery Siding {*Rothley Shield Quarry Siding
Ewesley	16	39	G P L H C	—	
Fontburn	17	45	P		{Whitehouse Siding {Ewesley Goods Siding
Brinkburn	21	79	G P H C		{Forestburn Siding {Brinkburn Colliery Siding
Rothbury	24	15	G P F L H C	4 tons	Shell's Warehouse

G = Goods; P = Passengers; F = Furniture, vans, motor cars etc.; L = Livestock;
H = Horses & prize cattle; C = Carriages & vehicles.
* = Sidings removed by turn-of-the-century.

Rothbury market and Donkin's sheep sales gave rise to some particularly heavy agricultural traffic, especially during the pre-Grouping period when Rothbury station was sometimes crammed with up to 100 cattle wagons. Scotsgap, too, was an important marketing centre, a large cattle mart being situated beside the station.

At the risk of stating the obvious, it may be necessary to add that the goods rolling stock seen on the Rothbury branch reflected the types of traffic carried, with wooden-bodied open wagons being much in evidence through-out the line's existence. Cattle wagons were also much in evidence through-out the NBR period, while general merchandise was carried in covered vans; most vehicles seen on the line were of NBR origin though consignments from the North Eastern or other companies sometimes brought 'foreign' wagons or vans onto the line.

There was, in general, just one freight working in each direction, and in 1906 this service departed from Rothbury at 10.40 am (after the engine had shunted in Rothbury yard for about 1 hour). The branch freight reached

Scotsgap at 11.40 am, and went forward to Morpeth at 1.15 pm; in the down direction, a return working left Morpeth at 3.45 pm and arrived back in Rothbury by 6.10 pm. On Mondays, a cattle train left Rothbury at 2.00 pm, and there was a return working from Rothbury to Scotsgap at 2.00 pm (MO). In addition, cattle wagons were regularly attached to passenger trains, while, if traffic was sufficiently heavy, the Reedsmouth passenger engine was pressed into service on special goods workings from Scotsgap to Morpeth or from Scotsgap to Rothbury.

The line was (1913) worked on the electric tablet system, the main crossing stations being Scotsgap and (to a lesser extent) Ewesley or Meldon. There were no two-platform passing stations anywhere on the line, but as there was no need for two passenger trains to pass en route this deficiency presented few problems. Contemporary maps show that there were no loops at Ewesley or Meldon, and it seems that when these stations were used as passing places by two goods trains (or one goods and one passenger working) one of the trains would have been shunted into a siding so that the other could pass.

When first opened in 1870 the Rothbury branch had only rudimentary signalling, but a degree of greater sophistication was subsequently introduced, with raised signal cabins at both Scotsgap and Rothbury. The other stations were signalled in a simpler way, most of the intermediate stopping places being equipped with up and down 'stop' signals – in some cases on a common post. Angerton, for example, was initially equipped with a single-posted station signal carrying two semaphore arms, though this archaic feature was subsequently replaced by separate signals at each end of the station.

In retrospect, the signalling provided between Scotsgap and Rothbury during the early part of the 20th century was probably over-elaborate in relation to likely traffic needs. Apart from market days, the line was busy only on Rothbury race days – on these occasions excursion stock was stabled in the goods sidings (or even sent back down the branch to Scotsgap). At other times the pace of life was so unhurried that trains were stopped so that the crew could set rabbit traps beside the line!

Pre-Grouping Locomotive Power

The North British Railway was initially worked by a bewildering variety of locomotive types, many of which were of doubtful quality. The company started to design its own engines during the 1860s, and by the following decade a modicum of standardisation had been achieved. Some of the older engines were successfully rebuilt and modernised, while capable locomotive superintendents such as Thomas Wheatley and Dugald Drummond introduced some outstanding new designs – among them the very first British inside-cylindered, inside-framed 4–4–0s (NBR Nos. 224 & 264). It is hard to ascertain, with any degree of precision, which locomotives were used on the Rothbury branch during its earliest days, but by analogy with other secondary lines it may have originally been worked by various outmoded main line types. If this supposition is correct one might reasonably assume that rebuilt Hawthorn or Dübs 2–2–2s or 2–4–0s appeared on the line at or around the time of its opening.

In a sense, recorded locomotive history on the Morpeth to Rothbury line begins with the introduction of Drummond's 'R' class 4–4–0Ts. Built at various times between 1880 and 1884, there were thirty of these diminutive engines, and the first 26 carried the names of places served by the NBR; No. 73 was called *Rothbury*, while sister engine No. 7 was dubbed *Morpeth*; both engines worked on the Rothbury line for many years.

Although the 'R' class 4–4–0Ts were extensively used on suburban duties, they were also used on rural branch lines, and this numerically-small class was destined to enjoy a long association with NBR border lines, becoming, in many ways, the classic local branch design (at least in the pre-Grouping era). These engines had 5 ft 0 in. coupled wheels and tiny, 2 ft 6 in. diameter leading wheels – the latter being solid, spokeless discs. Externally, the 'R' class locos sported typical 'Drummond' cabs, smokeboxes and boiler fittings, the overall effect being particularly attractive.

Goods traffic was handled by Holmes 0–6–0 goods locomotives, the familiar 'C' class being widely used during the NBR era. Introduced in 1888, the 'C' class 0–6–0s had 5 ft wheels and $18\frac{3}{4}$ in. × 26 in. cylinders; their weight was 41 tons 19 cwt. Several 'C' class engines are known to have worked on the Morpeth–Scotsgap–Rothbury route, among them Nos. 791, 797 and 779.

Like all NBR engines, the 'R' class 4–4–0Ts and 'C' class 0–6–0s carried the company's curiously-illusive livery which seemed, in some lights, to have been brown, and in others green! In reality this brownish-green colour scheme seems to varied in relation to the amounts of green, brown or yellow pigments employed. Under Dugald Drummond, NBR goods locomotives were usually olive green, and at the end of the NBR era many goods engines were painted in a plain black livery.

Post-Grouping Developments

In 1923 the North British Railway became an integral part of the newly-created London & North Eastern Railway under the provisions of the Transport Act 1921. In the short term, the 1923 grouping produced few major changes – one small innovation being the introduction of a standardised engine classification system based upon locomotive wheelbases. The new system was both logical and simple in that large Pacific engines were given the 'A' prefix, 4–6–0s became 'Bs', Atlantics became 'Cs' and so on. As there was usually more than one type of engine within each basic grouping, the new notations were further sub-divided by the addition of numerals denoting each class. Insofar as this new system concerned the Rothbury branch, the long-serving 'R' class 4–4–0Ts became LNER class 'D51', while the familiar Holmes 'C' class 0–6–0s were reclassified as LNER class 'J36'. These former North British classes continued to work on the branch until the mid-1920s, but thereafter, ex-North Eastern engines gradually assumed command of branch passenger and freight services.

In visual terms, the most noticeable aspect of the LNER takeover concerned the application of new, and somewhat uninspiring liveries. Small tank locomotives such as the ex-NBR 4−4−0Ts were given a simple black livery relieved only by red lining and bright yellow 'LNER' lettering, and in later years most LNER engines were painted unlined black (apple green livery being applied only to large passenger locos). Coaches were painted a drab brown colour, and although 'varnished teak' was adopted for new vehicles, few branch line coaches received this more expensive finish.

The LNER train service was merely a continuation of that provided in the NBR period. In July 1925, for example, trains left Rothbury for Morpeth at 8.09 am, 11.30 am and 4.24 pm, with corresponding return workings from the junction at 9.48 am, 2.15 pm and 5.50 pm respectively. An interesting feature of this post-grouping timetable concerned the provision of through coaches to Newcastle; these were available on the two morning up trains, while in the return direction travellers could ride through to Rothbury on the second and third down trains of the day. An additional train ran on Wednesdays and Saturdays, when an evening service was advertised from Rothbury at 8.30 pm, with a balancing down working from Morpeth at 9.50 pm. There were no Sunday services, and indeed, regular Sunday trains were never a feature of Rothbury branch operations.

Freight traffic was conveyed by a morning train which generally left Rothbury after the departure of the early morning passenger service, and in the 1920s this goods working departed at 8.32, arriving back at the terminus by 2.33 pm. This mode of operation necessitated the provision of two en-gines at Rothbury for passenger and goods services, and it had, for many years, been usual for one passenger tank and one 0−6−0 tender engine to be out-stationed at Rothbury.

In LNER days, the normal branch passenger locomotive was an ex-North Eastern Railway 'G5' 0−4−4T, while goods traffic was usually handled by ex-NER 'J21' 0−6−0s. Another locomotive used in LNER days, albeit on a less regular basis, was former NER 'F8' 2−4−2T No. 1599. Originally designed for suburban duties, No. 1599 belonged to a class of 60 engines that had been introduced as far back as 1886; the engine enjoyed a long association with the central Northumberland area, having been employed on the neighbouring Haltwhistle to Alston branch during the 1920s. Sister engine No. 1583 was stationed at Reedsmouth for use on the Wansbeck branch passenger service to and from Scotsgap, and in this capacity it is conceivable that the engine would have occasionally been commandeered for duties on Rothbury freight turns.

The Later LNER Period

In May 1936 Rothbury's allocation consisted of 'F8' 2−4−2T No. 1599 and a 'J21' 0−6−0, but the 2−4−2T had been replaced by the following month, and later in the summer an observer noted that the Rothbury branch train consisted of a 'G5' 0−4−4T and three ex-North British coaches.

The pattern of a 'G5' 0−4−4T for passenger work and an 0−6−0 for goods duties persisted throughout the 1930s, and in the early months of 1939 the branch engines comprised 'G5' 0−4−4T No. 2086 and 'J21' 0−6−0 No. 877. Meanwhile, Reedsmouth had remained an outpost of North British influence, and in the later 1930s its allocation included ex-NBR 'J36' 0–6–0s Nos. 9754, 9779 and 9791; these engines occasionally worked on the Rothbury line, and in the summer of 1939 'J36' No. 9754 was sent to Rothbury to replace 'G5' 0–4–4T No. 2086. (At least one of the LNER's steam railcars is believed to have run on the line, though not on a regular basis.)

Short wheelbase passenger vehicles were used on the Rothbury branch in the early years, but these archaic coaches were eventually replaced by bogie stock. The regular branch set was usually cleaned at Rothbury, a vacuum cleaner van being sent out to the terminus for this purpose. The latter vehicle was an ex-NER brake third, which was allocated to the Newcastle district and covered several other local branches (among them the Alston and Allendale lines).

The May 1930 Working Timetable provides a useful glimpse of the Rothbury branch in operation in the years before World War II. The times of arrival and departure were similar to those pertaining in 1925, with up workings from Rothbury at 8.09, 11.30 am and 4.24 pm and balancing return trips from Morpeth at 9.51 am, 2.15 and 5.50 pm. An extra train left Rothbury at 8.30 pm on Wednesdays and Saturdays only, the return working from Morpeth being at 9.50 pm. The daily freight train was booked to leave Rothbury at 8.32 am, while in the down direction a northbound goods train left Morpeth at 12.32 pm.

Notes appended to the timetable reveal that the 8.32 ex-Rothbury called as required at the intermediate sidings *en route* to Scotsgap, though on Mondays stone traffic was to be left at Scotsgap so that 'important wagons and live stock' could be worked through to Morpeth; any stone wagons left at Scotsgap were taken to Morpeth in the early afternoon by the 12.00 pm local freight from Reedsmouth Junction. A further note shows that the 9.51 am and 5.50 pm passenger trains from Morpeth to Rothbury were permitted to convey live stock wagons, 'subject to the regulations as to continuous brakes as contained in the general appendix'.

The outbreak of World War II in September 1939 resulted in a curtailment of branch train services, and an emergency wartime timetable brought into use on 2nd October, 1939 provided just two trains each way on the 24¼ mile route between Morpeth and Rothbury. In the up direction, passenger trains left Rothbury at 8.05 am and 4.25 pm, the balancing return trips from Morpeth being at 10.01 am and 5.45 pm respectively.

Basing their predictions upon the relatively high number of deaths that had been caused by World War I aeroplane and Zeppelin raids, British government 'experts' assumed that the *Luftwaffe* would drop around 950 tons of bombs a day, causing massive destruction and 2 million casualties within the first six months of war. There was widespread fear of a series of 'knock-out' blows on major cities such as Newcastle, and faced with this dreadful scenario the LNER sent as many spare locomotives as could be mustered to a number of secret dispersal points. One of these rural locations was Rothbury which, being far from major industrial targets, was considered to be safe from aerial attack. Meanwhile, a number of veteran locomotives from York Railway Museum had been sent to neighbouring Reedsmouth; the engines concerned included the Grand Junction Railway 2–2–2 *Columbine*,

Brighton 0–4–2 No. 214 *Gladstone*, and the Stourbridge-built 0–4–0 *Agenoria* (the sister of *Stourbridge Lion*, the first locomotive to run in America).

In May 1940, the fall of France led to fears of an imminent Nazi invasion of the British Isles, and at least one Rothbury-based engine was transferred to a somewhat larger 'reserve pool' at Alston – the latter place being more conveniently-situated in relation to the east and west coast main lines.

Happily, pre-war assessments of the effectiveness of German bombing turned out to be wildly inaccurate, and the *Luftwaffe* was unable to destroy any British cities or communications centres. Neither did the expected invasion take place, and when, in the summer of 1941, Hitler launched his long-planned attack on Russia, the first, critical phase of the war came to an end. In the next few years, Britain prepared for the eventual liberation of Europe, and like all British railway lines the Rothbury branch was called upon to handle a variety of extra traffic in connection with the continuing war effort. Although the Rothbury line served no large military installations, branch trains played a vital role in the conflict by carrying passenger and freight traffic that would otherwise have been sent by road – and with vital petrol supplies strictly rationed the importance of steam-powered railways soon became apparent!

Meanwhile, central government regulations had contributed to industrial changes as, in the search for greater efficiency, the local mining and quarrying industry was rationalised. Uneconomic pits had been closing since the early 1900s, and in November 1941 Greenleighton Drift Mine (near Longwitton) was officially abandoned. Its demise heralded the end of coal-mining in the Rothbury area – although the need for good quality stone for aerodrome construction and road-building ensured the survival of neighbouring Ewesley Quarry.

The basic wartime passenger service, with its sparse ration of two up and two down workings, was maintained throughout the emergency period, and in October 1946 – a year after the cessation of hostilities – local travellers were still offered a limited choice of one morning and one evening working between Rothbury and Morpeth. On Saturdays however, the branch train service was increased to four up and four down workings, an interesting feature of the 1946–47 timetable being the provision of a limited-stop return service from Morpeth at 10.50 am (SO). This working called at all stations on the Wansbeck line as far as Scotsgap (arr. 11.20), after which the train ran non-stop to Rothbury.

The end of the war in Europe had been followed, in June 1945, by the election of a Labour government pledged to nationalise rail transport and other important industries, and the new administration lost no time in putting these radical ideas into effect. At midnight on 31st December, 1947 the 'Big Four' railways companies set up under the provisions of the Transport Act 1921 were abolished, and thereafter the Rothbury branch passed into state control as part of an entirely new, nation-wide transport organisation known as 'British Railways'.

Chapter Four
The Route Described

Having sketched-in the history of the Rothbury branch from its inception until World War II, it would now be appropriate to look at the stations and route of this little-known line in greater detail, and the following section will take readers on a guided tour of the branch from Morpeth through to Rothbury. In general, the details that follow will be correct for the late LNER and early BR period around 1935–1952.

Morpeth

Morpeth, the eastern 'terminus' for Rothbury branch services, was a North Eastern station, although the North British company exercised running powers over the NER in order to reach the passenger station and goods yard. The station was laid-out on an approximate north-east to south-west axis, and the single track Wansbeck Valley route ran parallel to main line for a distance of about 20 yards before diverging westwards beyond the platforms.

Morpeth was, in the 1870s, the scene of two accidents, both of which took place near the divergence of the Wansbeck branch and the main line. The most serious of these mishaps occurred on the night of 18th March, 1877, when an up express from Edinburgh to London became derailed as it passed through the station. The train involved was the delayed 10.30 pm from Edinburgh and the cause of the derailment was later found to have been a loose fishplate – though there were suspicions that the express had been travelling faster than normal at the time of the accident. The train – headed by Fletcher 2–4–0 No. 901 and consisting of a dozen short-wheelbase passenger or luggage vehicles – passed through the station in safety, but as it passed the Wansbeck line, the engine left the rails and skidded to a halt on its side across the main line and branch; the tender careered across the Wansbeck route, and the wooden passenger vehicles crashed violently into the wrecked locomotive. Five travellers died in the accident and ten were injured – most of the casualities being in the front part of the train which had been telescoped by the sudden impact. The light of dawn revealed a scene of utter chaos, and for a time the main line and branch were completely blocked by the wreckage.

Commenting on the Morpeth disaster, Captain Tyler of the Board of Trade suggested that at least some of the injuries could have been avoided if the train had been fitted with continuous brakes, and in this context it is clear that an earlier accident at Morpeth in the 1870s would have been avoided altogether if the train concerned had been equipped with vacuum brakes. The incident, which took place on 15th September, 1872, involved a Rothbury branch working composed of several four-wheeled coaches. The train had just left Morpeth when, having commenced the long climb up to Meldon, one of its chain couplings parted and three passenger vehicles and a van ran back towards Morpeth where they collided with an oncoming freight train.

Morpeth itself was situated to the north of the station. An attractive old town, the settlement grew up around a strategic river crossing on the River

Class 'G5' 0–4–4T No. 67296 waits in the branch platform at Morpeth with a Rothbury one-coach service.   *W.A. Camwell*

Meldon station on the North British main line, between Morpeth and Scotsgap, as seen on a commercial postcard at the turn-of-the-century.   *Lens of Sutton*

Wansbeck, and in Medieval times it had both a castle and a Cistercian Abbey. Morpeth's most famous son was Admiral Cuthbert Collingwood, who had been second-in-command of the British fleet at the Battle of Trafalgar; his hobby (when not at sea) was said to have been planting acorns – an activity calculated to ensure that England never ran short of oak trees with which to build more battleships!

Meldon

Leaving Morpeth, branch trains ran due west along the Wansbeck Valley route for several miles, climbing steadily on a succession of rising gradients, the steepest of which were at 1 in 95 and 1 in 90. Meldon, the first stop, was 5 miles 31 chains from Morpeth; a typical Wansbeck Valley wayside station, it was situated in the middle of a prosperous farming area which, in the days before mass motor transport, had yielded much traffic for the railway. The station was fully-equipped with loading docks, and its booking office and waiting room were solidly-built of local stone. There was just one platform, on the north side of the running line, and a minor road was carried across the track at the western end of the station.

Meldon's track plan was relatively simple. The main goods siding was on the up (i.e. north) side of the line, and there was another long siding on the down side; both of these dead-end sidings were entered from the Scotsgap end. Two short spurs diverged from the main siding, but there were (in later years at least) no loop lines for use during shunting operations.

Angerton

From Meldon, the line climbed at 1 in 100 for a short distance before the route commenced a brief descent towards Angerton. Falling, first at 1 in 110 and then at 1 in 100, the route continued through pastoral scenery, and westbound trains soon reached the intermediate station at Angerton.

Situated some 7 miles 53 chains from Morpeth, Angerton was similar to Meldon. The station building was another stone-built design, featuring rectangular windows and a low-pitched slate roof. Built to the familiar 'L' plan, it incorporated a central booking hall and one cross wing – the wing being of two stories and containing domestic accommodation for the station master and his family; it had probably been designed by John Furness Tone, the Wansbeck Valley Engineer. Other facilities at Angerton included the usual goods yard, loading banks, and pens for livestock traffic. A minor road from Bolam to Hartburn crossed the line on the level at the western end of the station.

Middleton

Continuing westwards, the line descended at 1 in 70 towards the River Wansbeck, and having crossed from the south bank to the north side of the river on a 2-span bridge, the route resumed its climb. After a mile at 1 in 67½ the railway levelled-out for a very short distance, but the respite was only temporary, and Middleton, the next stopping place, was approached on another stretch of 1 in 67½ rising gradient.

Close-up view of the Scotsgap signal cabin, showing the all-stone construction of this ex-NBR box.　　　*J. Scott*

Ivatt 2−6−0 No. 46474 shunts the Rothbury branch pick-up freight at Scotsgap; the date is *circa* 1960. This view shows the other side of the signal box.

　　　W.S. Sellar

A general view of Scotsgap Junction station during the LNER period (probably c.1930). The original, single-storey signal cabin has now been adapted for use as a store. Note the bracket, lattice mast signals (*see page 93*).　　　　*Lens of Sutton*

Scotsgap station buildings from the rear. Note that the two-storey station master's house was a full cross wing, whereas the projecting portion at the front of the building was not a true cross wing.　　　　*R.M. Casserley*

A platform scene at Scotsgap around 1950; a class 'J21' 0–6–0 No. 65042 arrives with a single-coach train from Rothbury.

Ian Futers Collection

No. 65727, class 'J25', 0–6–0 seen here fitted with a snow plough passing through Scotsgap Junction in the early 1950s.
W.A. Camwell

Scotsgap Junction, looking west on 7th July, 1951, with No. 65035 arriving with the local pick-up goods service.
W.A. Camwell

Like its counterparts at Meldon and Angerton, Middleton was of Wansbeck Railway origin, but whereas the other intermediate stations between Morpeth and Scotsgap were provided with substantial, stone-built buildings, the tiny station at Middleton had simple wooden buildings of little architectural interest. The station was 9 miles 13 chains from Morpeth.

In Victorian days, Middleton had boasted a loop siding that could be shunted from either direction, but in the LNER period the track layout consisted of a single, dead-end siding facing Morpeth.

Beyond, the line climbed steadily at 1 in 67½ as it approached the hillier, more windswept terrain beyond Scotsgap. The scenery on this section of the line was wilder than that encountered earier, although the overall impression was of a pastoral, rather than a moorland landscape.

Scotsgap Junction

Scotsgap, the point at which the Northumberland Central Railway joined the earlier Wansbeck line, was poorly-equipped as a junction. There were no branch bays, and passenger facilities were confined to a single platform on the down side. The station building was solidly-built of local stone, and a hip-roofed signal box stood sentinel at the Morpeth end of the platform.

Scotsgap's track layout incorporated two parallel loops together with two sidings on the north side, and the resulting configuration provided five, more or less parallel lines. There were, in addition, three short spurs, one of which acted as a useful headshunt at the eastern end of the main loop while another gave access to a 42 ft diameter locomotive turntable. The outermost siding served a goods loading platform and an adjacent cattle market. A 2-ton yard crane was available for use when timber or other heavy loads were transferred between road and rail vehicles, and a goods warehouse provided covered accommodation for perishable or valuable forms of goods traffic.

In architectural terms, Scotsgap was clearly related to the other stations on the Wansbeck Valley route. The main station building, for instance, was very similar to Angerton, being, in effect, another 'L' plan structure (albeit with a second, subsidiary wing that did not in fact extend the full width of the main block). The station master's private accommodation occupied a two-storey cross wing at the eastern end of the building, while toilets and other facilities were situated in a group of single-storey extensions at the eastern extremity of the building. This substantial, stone-built structure was more or less devoid of decoration, though its otherwise severe facade was enlivened by the provision of prominent stone quoins. The main external walls were constructed of 'snecked' stonework (i.e. large and small blocks laid in interrupted courses) and the windows were of large-paned casement type.

Although of later construction than the station building, the signal cabin was of matching appearance, being built entirely of stone. It had a hipped, slated roof, and the operating floor was lit by casement windows. Other buildings at Scotsgap Junction included the usual assortment of huts and permanent way stores, together with a small water tower on the down side of the line. The latter structure was of brick construction, with a rectangular iron tank and a long horizontal pipe from which locomotives could take water by means of a flexible hose attached to one end; the water tower also incorporated a small coaling stage in its lower storey.

An an operational centre, Scotsgap Junction was of some importance in that it linked the Rothbury and Wansbeck Valley lines and here – at this otherwise remote place – travellers from Morpeth were able to change into connecting trains in order to complete their journeys to Reedsmouth or beyond.

Like other country stations, Scotsgap Junction had a succession of station masters over the years, one of the best-known being William Walker, who was in charge during the Edwardian era; an earlier station master, around 1890, was Hedley Fenwick Rutherford.

Leaving Scotsgap Junction, branch trains passed beneath the B6343 road, and with the turntable to the right and water tower to the left, the journey to Rothbury resumed. Rattling over a crossover, the panting 'G5' 0–4–4Ts and their veteran coaches left the 'main line' and immediately gained the Rothbury branch, which ran beside the Reedsmouth Junction route for the next half mile. Running on what appeared to be a double track route (but was in reality two single lines) trains passed beneath a characteristic North British wooden occupation bridge, beyond which the branch suddenly veered northwards, away from the main line.

Longwitton

Having gained their own route, trains passed through a shallow cutting before crossing the sparkling Hart Burn and a minor road in relatively quick succession. Climbing steadily at 1 in 73½, the railway was carried across the tiny Delf Burn, and with distant hills now visible from the carriage windows, the rising gradient eased slightly to 1 in 75. Northwards, the line passed beneath another overbridge, which was followed, soon afterwards, by a public road bridge carrying the B6342 road across the single line.

This southern extremity of the Rothbury line was the scene of an unfortunate accident that occurred on 5th July, 1875 – less than 3 years after the breakaway at Morpeth. Again, the cause of the accident seems to have been a broken coupling, though in this case the consequences were much worse in that an entire train was derailed. Contemporary newspapers such as the *Newcastle Daily Journal* refer, somewhat confusingly, to a 'connecting rod joining two wagons' which snapped as a morning up train was passing Donkin Crags (roughly mid-way between Scotsgap and Longwitton). The train involved consisted of six short-wheelbase passenger vehicles, eight empty stone wagons and at least two brake vans, and all of these vehicles were precipitated down a 30 ft embankment, resulting in death and injury to several travellers. Among the dead were Matthew Little, the guard, of Rothbury; George Shaw from Byker, a pattern-maker; William Fenwick, a mason from Shafto; and George Thompson, a contractor from Stanley (who died later in hospital at Morpeth). The injured included a joiner from Wallington, a painter from Morpeth, and the Reverend Kirsop, a Roman Catholic priest.

Inevitably, the death, and injuries sustained in this incident led to an outcry against the North British Railway, and the *Newcastle Daily Journal* went so far as to suggest that the company had something to hide. The largest pieces of wreckage were, claimed the paper, collected at Scots Gap, while combustible material was quickly burned; 'it seemed to be the design of the officers to destroy as much evidence as possible, and they were most jealous of the appearance of strangers'.

Passing the scene of this long-forgotten Victorian tragedy, trains maintained their northerly heading through increasingly wild terrain and, still climbing at 1 in 75, the route passed beneath an accommodation bridge before curving north-eastwards into the valley of the Ewesley Brook. Beyond, trains ran under the B6342 for a second time as they entered the first intermediate station at Longwitton.

Situated just 3 miles 24 chains from Scotsgap Junction, Longwitton was, in many ways, a typical Northumberland Central station. Built by a penurious (and dispirited company) this tiny Northumbrian stopping place consisted of little more than a wooden shack on a sleeper-and-cinder platform; to Victorian eyes such a station must have seemed hideously-plain, although 20th century industrial archaeologists would no doubt have been charmed by its quaint 'Emmett'-like features.

The station was situated in a shallow cutting, and the platform and goods yard were on the up side of the line. In later years, Longwitton's track layout was reduced to just one dead-end goods siding together with a short spur at the Rothbury end of the yard; there was no goods shed or yard crane, and the simple track layout was controlled by a ground frame. In earlier days, the station had served nearby quarries and coal mines, and, until the turn-of-the-century, two privately-owned mineral lines had diverged from the 'main line' to reach Longwitton limestone quarry and the Longwitton Colliery. These sidings had, however, disappeared by the 1920s and there were, by the 1950s, few reminders of these long-abandoned facilities.

In its late-Victorian heyday, Longwitton had been fully signalled, a small signal cabin being provided on the down side of the line. The track layout here was, after 1876, quite complicated, with a single dead-end siding on the up side and a loop siding to the south of the road bridge; the dead-end siding served Longwitton Colliery, while the loop siding was installed to serve the nearby quarry and limeworks.

The North British Railway carried out various modifications at Longwitton during the 1872–76 period. Board of Trade inspections were necessary before the new facilities could be brought into use, and an inspection report written by Lt Colonel Hutchinson on 23rd February, 1876 is of some interest insofar as it describes Longwitton station and sidings after the installation of the limeworks loop siding:

23rd February, 1876

Sir,

I have the honour to report, for the information of the Board of Trade, that, in compliance with the instructions contained in your minute of the 12th instant, I have inspected the arrangements in connection with the new siding junction at

A general view of Ewesley station looking from the north in July 1952. Note the grounded body used as additional storage alongside the station building. The track had been relaid with concrete sleepers. *C.J.B. Sanderson*

Longwitton station with similar grounded coachbody for storage purposes; again concrete sleepers have just been laid. *A.J. Wickens*

Ewesley station building was a wooden structure of utilitarian design standing on an earth-and-cinder platform; a Board of Trade inspection report dating from 1894 refers to an 'additional station building', suggesting that this small structure may have replaced an even simpler NCR building; alternatively, the station may have been extended by the NBR to provide increased accommodation for waiting travellers.

A.J. Wickens

The diminutive halt at Fontburn as seen on 15th February, 1952.   *C.J.B. Sanderson*

Longwitton on the Northumberland Central Railway branch of the North British Railway.

With the following exceptions, the arrangements have been satisfactorily carried out; the station arrangements have been much improved.

1) In consequence of facing points occuring at each end of the platform, starting signals should be provided, both for up and down trains, to ensure these points being right when trains are passing over them.

2) As the line where the limeworks loop is situated is on a falling gradient (towards Scotsgap) of 1 in 75, all down mineral trains should be locked into the sidings before commencing to do their work.

3) The facing points at the Scotsgap end of the limeworks loop have, in consequence of the altered position of the signal cabin, become too far from it (nearly 300 yards) to be safely worked by the signalman – it would be far better that these points should, if possible, be dispensed with altogether, but if this cannot be done they should be bolted . . . but not worked from the cabin.

The point guard at the facing points is not in order and should be looked at. The Board of Trade should be informed after these requirements have been complied with.

I have, etc.,

C.S. Hutchinson

In architectural terms, Longwitton was simple in the extreme, and the timber-framed, contractor's type station buildings would not have looked out of place in the Australian outback or in some other part of the distant Empire. The building incorporated the usual booking office and waiting room facilities, access from the platform being through two doorways. Three brick chimney stacks rose from the rear wall of the main block, and an old short-wheelbase passenger vehicle provided additional storage accommodation on the exposed platform. At night, the station was lit by oil lamps placed in simple glass lanterns – one of which was bolted to the front of the station building while the others were attached to upright wooden posts.

In earlier days, Longwitton was considered important enough to have its own station master, and Victorian or Edwardian editions of *Kelly's Directory of Northumberland* record many of their names. In 1914, for example, the local station master was John Davison. Prior to this, the station had been manned by a 'collector', who, though not a station master as such, was in charge of fare collection and day-to-day supervision of the station; one of these early 'collectors' was Peter Jamieson, who worked at Longwitton during the 1890s.

Interestingly, Longwitton had originated as a semi-private stopping place known as 'Rothley', which did not appear in the earliest timetables, but it was mentioned in the *Newcastle Daily Journal* opening-day report in November 1870 (*see Chapter Two*).

Ewesley

Departing from Longwitton, northbound trains dropped towards the Font Valley on a series of falling gradients. Passing beneath another overbridge, the railway maintained its north-easterly heading for a short distance before curving leftwards in a great arc which brought the route onto a north-westerly alignment.

Ewesley, the next stopping place, was 5 miles 28 chains from Scotsgap. Like Longwitton, it was a simple, single platform station; the single-siding goods yard and station buildings were on the up side, and there was an additional dead-end siding on the down side of the line. Curiously, the station was built in the very centre of a circular earthwork or 'camp', and traces of this archaeological feature could be discerned on both sides of the line; the B6342 passed beneath the railway at the southern end of the platform.

The station building was more substantial than that of Longwitton; of timber construction, it had a gabled roof, and provided the usual booking office and waiting room facilities. The platform was fenced with vertical paling, and at night the station was illuminated by oil lamps.

There was, in addition to the station building, a separate station master's house. Of distinctly 'Scottish' appearance, this diminutive dwelling was situated behind the platform on the up side of the line – in which position the occupant could keep a watchful eye on the nearby station building! The station was, at one time, protected by a rudimentary signalling system consisting of up and down home and distant signals worked from a small 8-lever cabin on the platform; these were, however, subsequently removed. The only other structure on the earth-and-cinder platform was a small lock-up or store which, from its general appearance, had probably started life as a short-wheelbase passenger vehicle.

Like the other intermediate stations en route to Rothbury, Ewesley was little more than a staffed halt, but in NBR days it was treated as a 'full' station under the control of its own station master. In 1887, for example, Hannah Thornton served as station mistress at this isolated NBR outpost, while on the eve of World War I the local station master was Samuel Hunter.

Once a block post on the 13 mile single line between Scotsgap and Rothbury, Ewesley was the only crossing station on the Northumberland Central section. There was little need for passing to take place – the branch being so lightly used that up and down workings rarely met en route. When, however, traffic was sufficiently heavy, Ewesley could be pressed into service as a passing place, its long down siding being utilised as a refuge loop for goods trains. This siding was laid in 1894 and it was 'passed' by Major Marindin of the Board of Trade on 11th August; his BoT inspection report referred to 'a new siding ... facing down trains' that was 'worked from a cabin containing 8 levers'. The major also referred, somewhat ambiguously, to an 'additional station building' that had been ordered but not yet erected; this may have been the simple goods lock-up on the platform (though it is possible that the main station building was rebuilt under NBR auspices around 1890).

Ewesley itself was situated within easy walking distance of the railway, though this unimportant hamlet can have contributed little traffic, apart from occasional consignments of sheep or wool.

Fontburn Halt

From Ewesley, trains ran downhill for a short distance before reaching a brief stretch of rising gradients. Curving imperceptibly northwards, the line crossed over the River Font on the Fontburn viaduct; to the left, travellers could obtain a good view of Fontburn reservoir.

The viaduct was an impressive structure, with twelve 30 ft spans and a maximum height of around 60 ft above local ground level. It was flanked by lofty embankments, which had given much trouble during the construction of the railway during the 1860s.

Fontburn Halt was situated a short distance beyond the viaduct, at 6 miles 34 chains. Once a focus for several coal and mineral lines, Fontburn was, in later years, a simple unstaffed stopping place offering rudimentary facilities for the occasional traveller.

Fontburn's importance stemmed from the proximity of Whitehouse Lime-works, which predated the railway and was said to have been used during the building of the nearby viaduct. The lime works was served by two dead end sidings that branched from the running line near the passenger platform to reach the kilns, and a connecting tramway ran eastwards from the kilns towards Whitehouse (later Ewesley) quarries. Another siding extended northwards near the junction with the main line, and this provided a convenient interchange point with a short tramway from the neighbouring Whitehouse Colliery.

Like Longwitton, Fontburn was developed by the North British Railway during the 19th century, sidings being added at intervals over a period of about 18 years. Until 1884, there had been no facilities whatsoever at this remote place, but in that year the NBR installed a siding connection on the east side of the single line. The siding, which faced towards Rothbury, was entered via a single turnout, a small ground frame being provided to work the junction points. When first installed, the new line was arranged as a loop, but the layout was subsequently amended to form the two dead-end sidings mentioned above. Maps dating from 1884 show two 'proposed lime kilns' near the southern extremity of the siding, and the short 'catch siding' (that later served Whitehouse Colliery) was shown as a hatched line – indicating that it had not then been laid.

The new limeworks siding was inspected by Major-General (formerly Lt Colonel) C.S. Hutchinson of the Board of Trade on 29th November, 1884 and, as usual, the resulting BoT report contained much useful data relating to the operation and physical appearance of Fontburn at that time. As usual, the report began with an elegant introduction, and the Major-General then made two detailed recommendations relating to the day-to-day working of the siding:

29th November, 1884

Sir,
I have the honour to report, for the information of the Board of Trade, that, in compliance with the instructions contained in your minute . . . I have inspected a new siding junction between Ewesley and Brinkburn stations on the Northumberland Central section of the North British Railway.

The point and signal arrangements for the junction have been properly carried out, but, as the gradient of the main line falls sharply from the junction towards Ewesley, the company must give an undertaking to take any train proceeding from Ewesley to Brinkburn having work to do at the siding off the main line before any shunting commences, and to confine all the shunting in the siding.

To enable such an undertaking to be properly carried out, the dead end of the siding must be lengthened some 20 yards towards Brinkburn.

Subject to these requirements, and to the receipt of a satisfactory undertaking re. use of the new siding junction, the . . . new siding may be sanctioned.

I have, etc.,
C.S. Hutchinson
(Major General)

The Major-General's reference to the 'dead end of the siding' being extended towards Brinkburn is puzzling because the buffer stops at the southern extremity of the new line actually faced the *other* way towards Ewesley! The inspector probably meant to say that a shunting neck was needed at the Brinkburn end of the siding so that, when goods vehicles were positioned in the limeworks, the engine would not have to foul the main line. (If this supposition is correct, the 'catch siding' that was added near the junction points would have fulfilled the inspector's requirements).

Fontburn Halt did not exist in 1884, but the limeworks siding was protected by distant signals and by a 'stop' signal with two arms on one common post; these were worked from a small ground frame on the western side of the running line (later moved to the opposite side of the track).

Fontburn did not appear in NBR timetables until the early 1900s, but it is likely that trains called on a semi-official basis during the 19th century; (there was no proper road access to Whitehouse Quarry or lime works, and it is reasonable to assume that local workmen would have reached their places of employment by train). Contemporary 25 in. Ordnance Survey maps show what appears to be a short platform near Whitehouse Quarry sidings, and on this evidence it seems likely that a simple halt may have been in use at least as early as 1896.

Further traffic was brought to Fontburn around 1900, when Fontburn Reservoir was constructed to the west of the railway, and a special siding was added to handle construction materials. This new siding, on the down side of the line, was inspected by the BoT on 29th July, 1902; the inspection report stated that the siding 'in connection with Tynemouth Waterworks' faced Rothbury, and was worked by a 4-lever ground frame. There was no mention of a platform for passenger traffic – although considerable numbers of workmen may have been travelling to and from the construction site at that time.

The halt at Fontburn must, however, have been opened to traffic within the next few months because, by 1904, it was being shown in *Bradshaw* and in North British public timetables as an official stopping place for passenger trains. Thereafter the station remained in being as an unstaffed halt, and successive editions of the *Railway Clearing House Handbook of Stations* list Fontburn as a passenger-only station – the associated Whitehouse Siding being shown (confusingly) as 'Ewesley Siding' because it served Ewesley Quarry.

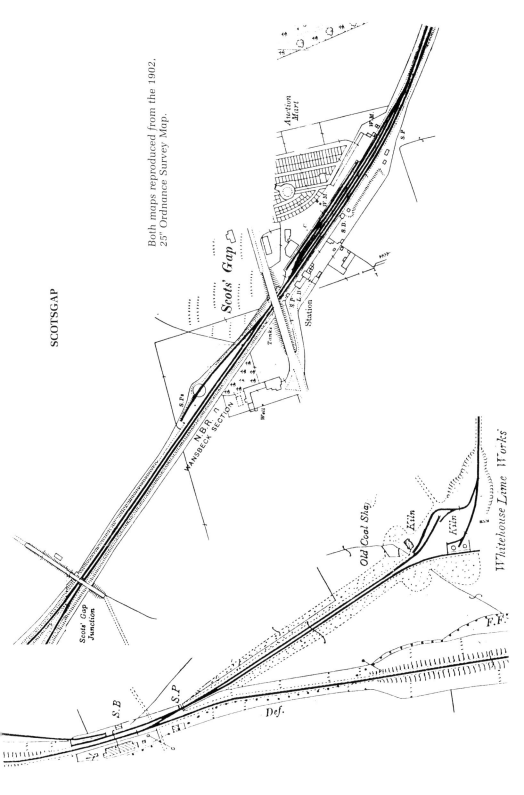

SCOTSGAP

Both maps reproduced from the 1902.
25" Ordnance Survey Map.

Scots' Gap

Auction Mart

Station

N.B.R.

WANSBECK SECTION

Scots' Gap Junction

S.B.

S.P

Def.

Old Coal Shed

Kiln

Kiln

Whitehouse Lime Works

F.F.

BRINKBURN

*The map is reproduced from the 1902, 25"
Ordnance Survey Map.*

The more substantial (and newly painted)
station building of Brinkburn, as seen from
the south on 16th July, 1962. *C.J.B. Sanderson*

Class 'G5' 0–4–4T No. 67296 draws into
Brinkburn station with a one-coach train.
Note the NBR-type wooden overbridge and
the tiny goods lock-up (*left*). The shed
between the goods store and the station
building was once a lever cabin.

W.A. Camwell

Leaving Fontburn, branch trains ran northwards, through cuttings, to Forestburn (19 miles 38 chains) where a further colliery tramway brought coal from neighbouring collieries. Beyond, the railway continued to Brinkburn Colliery Siding, at which point a similar tramway conveyed coal from the Lee Colliery, just over a mile to the east. The embankments and other earthworks on this section of the NCR line were impressive, some of the banks being around 50 ft high; it is said that over 100,000 cubic yards of earth was removed from the Forestburn area during the construction of the railway.

Brinkburn

Continuing northwards trains coasted down into the Coquet Valley on a succession of falling gradients, the steepest of which was 1 in 60; as mentioned earlier, John Furness Tone had not intended to use such steep gradients, but they had nevertheless been sanctioned at a later stage of construction as a means of saving money.

With the Simonside Hills rising to over 1,400 ft on the left hand side of the line, trains continued their descent towards Rothbury, Brinkburn, the penultimate station, being approached on a 1 in 75 falling gradient. Situated on a curve, Brinkburn was 10 miles 68 chains from Scotsgap. Another simple, single-platform station, it consisted of a short platform on the up side of the line, with a small station building and a tiny corrugated iron goods lock-up.

The simple station building was similar to that at Ewesley, being a timber framed structure, clad in vertical weather boarding with narrow 'cover strips' affixed along the joints. The roof was slated, and two brick chimney stacks protruded through the ridge tiles.

Other buildings at Brinkburn included a small wooden hut that had once functioned as a signal cabin, and a single-storey station master's dwelling house. Nearby, a moorland track was carried over the single line on a typical North British-style wooden bridge. There was just one goods siding on the up side; this faced towards Rothbury and could only be shunted by down trains.

Platform fittings included the usual glass lanterns and a station seat with the name 'BRINKBURN' painted on its back-rest. The platform was fenced with pale-and-space fencing like that at neighbouring Ewesley, and there were, at one time, up and down home signals at each end of the station – the down home being on the southern side of the wooden overbridge, while the up signal was immediately north of the goods yard turnout. The staffing arrangements at Brinkburn resembled those found elsewhere on the branch – that is to say, in North British days the station was fully staffed with its own station master, whereas in later years it became little more than a halt.

Rothbury

Leaving Brinkburn, northbound trains entered what was, perhaps, the most attractive part of their route. With the River Coquet now clearly visible on the right hand side of the line, the route passed through a narrow defile which, in the Spring or early Summer, was enlivened by flowering rhododendrons and other colourful plants. With wooded hills now visible on all sides, the line wound its way along a narrow ledge, and with Rothbury only a short distance further on, trains surmounted a short stretch of rising gradient on the approaches to the terminus. Beyond, the line dropped once again at 1 in 75, the final entry to Rothbury station being on the level.

Situated some 13 miles 4 chains from Scotsgap and 24 miles 15 chains from the start of the journey at Morpeth, Rothbury was a classic rural branch terminus, with most of the facilities usually found at the 'country' end of a single line. Its track plan consisted of a series of parallel loops, from which dead-end sidings diverged on both sides. The goods yard contained three sidings, one serving a small goods shed and another running beside a large cattle dock. The main running line ended on a 42 ft turntable, the layout being such that incoming engines had to run onto the table prior to running round their trains; a spur from the turntable led directly into the single road engine shed, while another ran into permanent way sheds in which platelayers' trolleys were stored.

Passenger facilities were concentrated on a single platform on the up (i.e. north) side of the line. The wooden station building was a semi-prefabricated structure of recognizable North British design, suggesting that the NBR had rebuilt the station at some time after the 1872 amalgamation. An 'H'-plan building, it featured prominent external panelling with the intervening spaces filled with vertical match boarding. The platform frontage was protected by a projecting canopy that extended the full length of the building, and boasted elaborate fretwork decoration.

Other buildings at Rothbury were of a varied nature, and included a signal box, a weigh-house and an ancient ex-NBR coach body which, like its counterpart at Longwitton, functioned as a store. The engine shed was a simple brick building with timber gables and a lean-to office; nearby, a miniature water tower provided watering facilities for the branch engines – a flexible hose being available for filling loco tanks. The tower was built of stone, and it abutted the engine shed in a somewhat untidy fashion – the two structures being, in effect, part of the same 'L' shaped building.

Rothbury's track plan incorporated one or two unusual features, notably the way in which the running line ended on the turntable. The trackwork at the goods yard throat was somewhat complicated, a cluster of turnouts being provided in a relatively small area; this complexity was probably needed to obviate shunting problems on the curved approaches to the terminus, though there may also have been a requirement to separate the goods lines from the main running line (i.e. to ensure that passenger trains did not have to negotiate too many turnouts as they arrived or departed from the station).

There was ample provision for stone and mineral traffic, the goods yard being, in effect, one vast loading dock. It was usual, on Rothbury race days, for part of this raised loading area to be used for passenger traffic. Indeed, the goods yard seems to have been treated as a sort of excursion station, and in recognition of this fact, the North British decided to formalise the situation by adapting part of the goods yard for passenger usage. Various alterations were carried out in 1899, the main innovation at that time being the removal of a crossover to a new position near the southern end of the station. This produced a much-lengthened passenger line, and an adjacent loading bank was, at the same time, transformed into a 'proper' excursion platform for race traffic.

The new arrangements at Rothbury were inspected by Major Francis Marindin of the Board of Trade on 14th October, 1899, the resulting BoT reported being as follows:

> Sir,
>
> I have the honour to report for the information of the Board of Trade that, in compliance with the instructions contained in your minute of 7th June 1899, I have inspected the alterations at Rothbury terminal station on the North British Railway.
>
> These alterations comprise a new facing point connection, the removal of an old one, and the shifting of some siding connections; and the practical result has been . . . to make available for passenger use a long loading bank hitherto used occasionally by excursion trains in a manner not satisfactory.
>
> The signal cabin contains 23 working levers. Number 15 disc should be worked by an independent lever or be dispensed with altogether.
>
> Subject to the satisfaction of these requirements, I can recommend that the use of the alterations at Rothbury may be sanctioned.
>
> I have the Honour to be,
Sir,
Your servant,
F. Marindin

Plans prepared in connection with the 1899 inspection reveal that the terminus had (for all intents and purposes) reached its final form, and there would be few changes in the years ahead – other than the routine renewal of time-expired rails and sleepers. In this context it may be worth adding that the original single-headed rail was soon replaced by conventional bull-head rails resting in cast iron chairs, though sections of the original 60 lb. per yard permanent way material may have survived for several years in out-of-the-way parts of the goods yard.

The station was fully signalled with the usual home and starter arms, the down home being a bracket assembly with one main arm and two subsidiary arms for incoming goods trains. Similarly, the up starting signal featured a bracketed subsidiary arm to regulate movement out of the goods yard. Both of these signals incorporated lattice posts.

Rothbury was, in many ways, a more important terminus than one might have expected; it was certainly a more impressive station than its counterparts at Longwitton, Ewesley, Fontburn or Brinkburn, with relatively lavish siding accommodation for livestock and other forms of goods traffic. The station was lit by gas for many years, but electric lighting was later installed – a refinement undreamt-of elsewhere on the bucolic NCR line! The lights in question were affixed to unusually slender uprights that also carried telephone wires.

One of Rothbury's first station masters was James Barrie, who was in charge of the terminus during the 1880s. By 1914, however, the station master was John Walker – perhaps a relative of William Walker, who served at Scotsgap Junction at that time. Other locally-based railway staff included porters, signalmen, booking clerks, locomotive crews and at least one guard, together with several permanent way men.

Rothbury's most famous inhabitant was probably Lord Armstrong, the arms manufacturer, whose Elswick Works in Newcastle eventually employed over 20,000 men. In 1863, Sir William Armstrong (as he then was) purchased an area of land in the township of Debdon, and in the next few years this energetic Victorian inventor created a large country house known as Cragside, the architect Norman Shaw being involved in the project from 1869 onwards. Sir William does not seem to have been actively involved in the promotion of the Northumberland Central Railway, but Cragside (which was near Rothbury station) was specially opened to celebrate the inauguration of the branch in November 1870.

Bradshaw's Timetable for October 1946.

British Railways passenger timetable for June 1951.

The RCTS/SLS special seen here at Rothbury terminus on 29th September, 1963 headed by '4MT' class 2−6−0 No. 43129.

J. Edgington

Snow plough-fitted class 'J25' 0−6−0 No. 65727 poses for the camera beside Rothbury station building. Introduced by the NER in 1898, these Worsdell-designed engines were similar to the 'J21s', but their smaller wheels made them more suitable for freight duties.

E.E. Smith

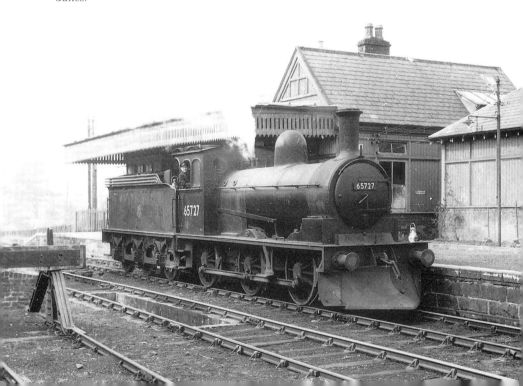

An unusual view of Rothbury this time looking towards the turntable. Note the water tower and grounded coach body.   *W.S. Sellar*

The water tower and locomotive pit, with catch-point protection for the turntable are clearly seen in this 13th April, 1957 view of the terminus. Class 'J21' 0−6−0 No. 65110 has just arrived with a race-goers special.   *E.E. Smith*

Class 'J21' 0−6−0 No. 65103 on the turntable at Rothbury terminus, c. 1950, photo-graphed from the doorway of the engine shed. *F.W. Hampson*

Ivatt class '2MT' 2−6−0 No. 46474 draws a rake of ventilated vans out of the goods sidings at Rothbury. The stone-built signal cabin can be seen to advantage as can the signal post and support posts. *W.S. Sellar*

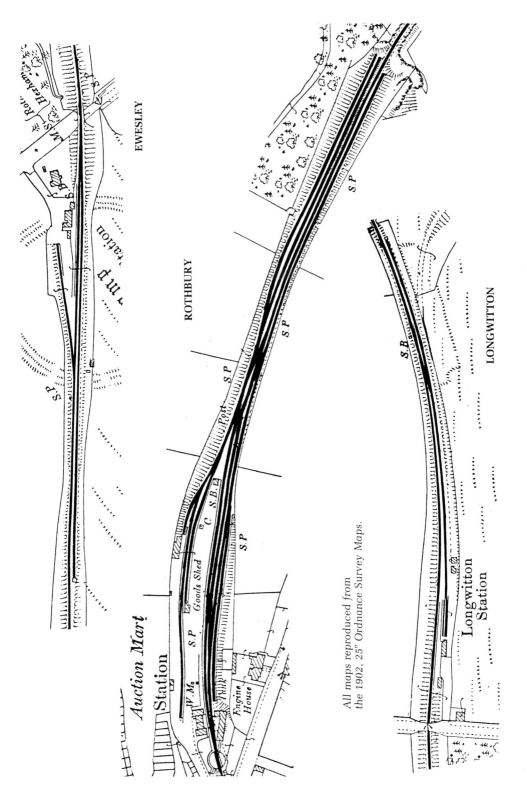

EWESLEY

ROTHBURY

LONGWITTON

Auction Mart

Station

S.P.

W.M.

Goods Shed

C S.B.

Engine House

S.P.

S.P.

S.P.

S.P.

Post

S.P.

S.B.

Longwitton
Station

All maps reproduced from
the 1902, 25" Ordnance Survey Maps.

A view of the turntable area at Rothbury. Although taken after closure, this shows the rail-served PW store (*left*) to advantage. *Ian Futers Collection*

A general view of Rothbury station, probably taken in the early 1930s, and looking towards the turntable. The white-washed edge of the platform marks the end of the original 'short' platform, the site of the first crossover (marking the end of the loop) being in the foreground. In 1899 the loop was extended and an area hitherto used mainly for goods traffic was brought into use as an excursion platform.

LRGP Collection

A further view of Rothbury station on the last day of scheduled passenger operation. Class 'J21' 0−6−0 No. 65035 shunts its train of cattle wagons and fitted goods vans. Note the yard crane. *J.W. Armstrong*

The crew of the last regular passenger train pose beside their locomotive on 13th September, 1952; note the incorrect dates on the headboard! *J.W. Armstrong*

Chapter Five
The British Railways Era (1948–1966)

The immediate results of nationalisation were remarkably few, and, as in 1923 the only obvious sign that a momentous change of ownership had in fact taken place concerned the liveries of locomotives and rolling stock. The varnished teak of the LNER was replaced by a striking new red and cream livery or (in the case of non-corridor vehicles) by plain maroon, while locomotives classified as 'mixed traffic' engines were given LNWR-type lined black livery.

When freshly applied these new colour schemes looked much brighter than the dreary blacks and browns of the preceding LNER era, though in practice it took months (even years) before the older liveries were replaced. Moreover, not all of the 'mixed traffic' engines received the new liveries, and the 'J21' 0–6–0s (which continued to work local freight services between Morpeth, Scotsgap and Rothbury) remained in plain, unadorned black livery.

Apart from the new liveries, the Morpeth to Rothbury line looked much the same as it had done in the LNER era, and in the late 1940s this former North British route was still worked by locomotives which, in most cases, had been built in the pre-grouping period! Trains were, in these final years of passenger operation, usually formed of just one brake third.

Post-Nationalisation Motive Power

Former North Eastern 'G5' 0–4–4Ts and 'J21' 0–6–0s were still hard at work on the Rothbury branch during the British Railways period, typical numbers, around 1950, being 'G5' 0–4–4Ts Nos. 67295, 67296 and 67341, together with 'J21' 0–6–0s Nos. 65035, 65103 and 65110. Other engines seen on the line during the post-war years included 'J27' 0–6–0s Nos. 65794, 65869 and 65882, and 'J25' 0–6–0 No. 65727. A summary of some of the varied motive power seen on the Rothbury branch is given on the following table – which also includes sample numbers for the benefit of potential modellers.

Table 2
MOTIVE POWER USED ON THE ROTHBURY BRANCH c.1900–1952

Class	Typical Numbers
Drummond D51 class 4–4–0T	1401/1402
Holmes J36 class 0–6–0	9797
G5 class 0–4–4T	67295/67296/67323/67328/67340/67341
J21 class 0–6–0	65032/65035/65075/65090/65110/65119
J25 class 0–6–0	65727/65675
Standard class 3MT 2–6–0	77011
J27 class 0–6–0	65789/65834/65842/65860/65891/65882
F8 class 2–4–2T	1583/1599
Ivatt class 2MT 2–6–0	46472/46473/46474/46482
Stanier class 3MT 2–6–2T	40075

The Last Years

The post-war years were a period of acute decline for rural lines throughout the British Isles, and with more and more travellers turning to road transport, it was clear that many branch lines were becoming hopelessly uneconomic. The future for the lightly-used ex-NBR lines from Morpeth to Reedsmouth and Rothbury was especially bleak, the main problem being lack of passenger traffic. This problem stemmed, in great part, from simple geographical factors; the Rothbury area had never been a heavily-populated region, and Rothbury (the only 'large' settlement in the vicinity) had a static population of less than 2,000.

In purely economic terms, there could be no real justification for the retention of the Rothbury branch – though the route continued to fulfil a valuable role as a winter lifeline to isolated communities that would otherwise have been cut-off in the severe Northumberland winters. The importance of these rural lines was underlined during the Arctic winter of 1947, when great efforts were made to keep the railways in operation – indeed, the Wansbeck section was the scene of an interesting (if somewhat desperate) experiment in which Whittle gas turbine engines were used to burn through the snow drifts!

In 1951 the Morpeth to Rothbury route was served by a skeleton service of just two up and two down trains. The morning up train left Rothbury at the early hour of 7.51 am and arrived at Morpeth an hour later at 8.51 am. A down working left Morpeth at 10.10 am and reached Rothbury at 11.18 am, and there was then a long gap until the departure of the second up service at 4.30 pm. The balancing down working departed from Morpeth at 5.50 pm and arrived back in Rothbury at 6.58 pm. Goods services consisted of a single round trip from Rothbury to Scotsgap, Morpeth and thence to Reedsmouth Junction.

Although Brinkburn station had been officially reduced to unstaffed halt status, there was little attempt to operate the branch on a cost-efficient basis, and the meagre train service of two passenger and one freight working still called for two locomotives to be out-stationed at Rothbury. In retrospect, it is clear that no real attempt was being made to run the Rothbury branch economically, and inevitably, the route became an early victim of rationalisation.

Passenger services between Morpeth, Scotsgap, Reedsmouth and Rothbury were withdrawn with effect from Monday 15th September, 1952, the last trains running on Saturday 13th. The final passenger service was worked by 'G5' 0–4–4T No. 67341, an appropriate headboard being carried on this melancholy occasion. No. 67341 was adorned with floral wreaths for the last journey, though, curiously, the opening date shown on the 'last day' headboard was incorrect, the wording being:

CHEERIO

ROTHBURY

1872 ——————————— 1952

GOOD

LUCK

Perhaps surprisingly, the withdrawal of passenger services did not entail total abandonment of the Rothbury line because freight traffic was still catered for – moreover, this ex-North British route still saw occasional passenger workings in connection with agricultural shows and other events. On 20th September, 1952, for instance, two separate excursions ran over the Morpeth to Scotsgap line *en route* to Bellingham. These trains – which traversed the Wansbeck line just 1 week after its formal closure – came from Blyth and Newbiggin, the excursion from Blyth being worked by 'J21' 0–6–0 No. 65042, while the one from Newbiggin was headed by sister engine No. 65110.

The Final Phase

Rothbury shed was closed in September 1952, and thereafter motive power for the surviving goods services was supplied by Blyth shed; the last engines shedded at Rothbury had been 'G5' 0–4–4T No. 67341 and 'J21' 0–6–0 No. 65035. The next few years produced few changes on the motive power front, and former NER 'J21' 0–6–0s continued to work the Rothbury branch freight turns. There were, from time to time, occasional visits by other locomotive classes; snow plough-fitted 'J25' 0–6–0 No. 65727, for instance, worked on the line around 1960, while sister engine No. 65675 also appeared on the branch on an irregular basis.

To laymen, the sight of a 'J25' 0–6–0 at the head of the Rothbury branch freight would hardly have constituted real variety – the 'J25s' were, after all, more or less identical to the familiar 'J21s' (apart from their smaller wheels and splashers). Tank engines, in contrast, were visibly different machines, and in this context it is interesting to record the appearance of ex-LMS Stanier class '3MT' 2–6–2T No. 40075 on the Morpeth to Rothbury and Reedsmouth line in November 1960. It was hoped that these relatively modern 'tankies' would be able to replace the venerable North Eastern Railway 0–6–0s that had dominated local freight operations since the 1930s, but sadly the LMS prairie tank was unsuitable, and on 12th November it was sent light to York. The days of pre-grouping motive power were nevertheless drawing to a close, and in the early 1960s the Rothbury line was typically worked by Ivatt class '2MT' 2–6–0s Nos. 46472, 46473, 46474 or 46482.

Another class seen on the branch around 1960–62 were the British Railways Standard class '3MT' 2–6–0s; on 21st June, 1962, for example, No. 77011 worked the 10.05 am local freight from Morpeth to Rothbury. At that time the train ran thrice weekly, Rothbury being served on Tuesdays, Thursdays and Fridays while on Mondays, Wednesdays and Fridays a similar working served Reedsmouth and Bellingham.

The Rothbury branch never became a diesel stronghold, but two class '08' shunters were once noted on a weed-killing train. Even more unusual was the sight of a 'J72' class 0–6–0T – one of the Newcastle station pilots – at the head of an Engineer's inspection train; 'J72s' were never associated with the line during its passenger-carrying days, and it was, perhaps, ironic that a member of the class should have traversed the branch towards the very end of its life.

Passenger trains did not entirely disappear after the cessation of regular services in 1952, and there were in fact several recorded instances of passenger working on the branch after that date. In the early 1950s the former NBR lines in Northumberland were often used by scenic excursions from the Newcastle area, a typical itinerary being Newcastle to Hexham via the Newcastle & Carlisle line, then Hexham to Reedsmouth over the Border Counties route followed by a final leg via Rothbury and thence to Morpeth. Such an excursion ran on 16th August, 1953, the motive power, on this occasion, being 'J21' class 0–6–0 No. 65110. A similar scenic tour took place on 23rd August, the engine being 'J21' No. 65090; both of these trains were composed of five bogie coaches.

Further scenic specials traversed the Rothbury branch on 14th August and 21st August, 1955, also on 12th August and 19th August, 1956, 'J21' 0–6–0 No. 65103 being a regular performer on these well-filled excursion trips from Newcastle; another 'J21' noted on one of the 1955 excursions was No. 65090. A race goers' special worked through to Rothbury on 13th April, 1957 and, as in previous years, the motive power was another 'J21' 0–6–0 – in this case No. 65110 from Heaton shed (52B).

At a time when rural branch lines were being closed in increasing numbers throughout the British Isles, railway enthusiasts belatedly discovered the existence of the North British 'English' lines, and with final closure to all traffic on the horizon, the Wansbeck and Rothbury lines started to attract their share of enthusiasts' specials. On 29th September, 1963, for example, Rothbury was visited by a Railway Correspondence & Travel Society Special hauled by Ivatt class '4MT' 2–6–0 No. 43129 – while diesel multiple unit specials traversed the NBR lines from Morpeth on several occasions.

A final steam-hauled special visited the Rothbury line on 9th November, 1963, and this enthusiasts' excursion was the last-but-one passenger train ever to run on the branch from Scotsgap Junction. The very last train (as far as can be ascertained) was a privately-arranged diesel working that traversed the route in July 1964, carrying members of the North Eastern Region's Chief Civil Engineering staff on their annual office outing.

The early 1960s were the 'Beeching era', and it was perhaps inevitable that the Morpeth–Scotsgap–Rothbury route would be closed in its entirety. The rural branch lines of Northumberland were slowly being dismembered, and, looking back on that fateful period, it becomes painfully clear that most of the damage occurred in a ten-year period lasting from 1956 until 1966; in that decade of closure and retraction the North British lines in Northumberland were simply wiped off the railway map.

A Decade of Closures

The neighbouring Border Counties line between Hexham, Reedsmouth and Riccarton Junction had survived as a passenger and freight route until October 1956, and as a freight-only line until September 1958. The Hexham to Reedsmouth and Bellingham to Riccarton sections were closed altogether in September 1958, leaving a residual section between Reedsmouth and Bellingham which was worked as an extension of the Wansbeck Valley route from Morpeth. In 1963, a further cut-back resulted in Woodburn (the site of a military establishment) becoming the end of the line from Morpeth.

The Scotsgap Junction to Rothbury line was finally closed to all traffic in November 1963, and the route was lifted in the following year. This withdrawal left the Morpeth–Scotsgap–Woodburn line in splendid isolation as the last remaining section of the North British Railway 'English' lines in central Northumberland, and it was perhaps appropriate that the official 'last' train over these lines was a steam-worked passenger excursion which ran from Newcastle to Scotsgap and Woodburn on Sunday 2nd October, 1966. Organised by the Gosforth Round Table, this historic working consisted of 11 maroon corridor coaches hauled by Ivatt class '4MT' 2–6–0s No. 43000 and 43063 coupled tender-to-tender for the out and back journey to Woodburn.

It is tempting to claim that the total eclipse of the railway system in central Northumberland was 'progress', but this conclusion is perhaps open to question. When one considers the gross inefficiency of road transport, with its high cost in terms of pollution and human life, the case for rail transport becomes very persuasive. Having said that, the NBR lines in Northumberland were built, not because the nation needed them, but because one private company was seeking to gain an advantage over its rivals. The lines in question were, in effect, unplanned, and once built, they received very little investment to make them more efficient. The LNER was too poor to bring the Rothbury branch and its neighbours up to modern standards, and in the 1950s and 1960s (by which time the former NBR lines had passed into state ownership) the government of the day was more interested in closing railways than in modernising them.

By 1960, the Rothbury branch had become an anachronism, and given the circumstances outlined above, its ultimate demise could never have been averted. One regrettable aspect of all this is, however, the fact that given just a few years more, the branch might have attracted the attention of preservationists who, with volunteer labour, could have revived this highly scenic line as a tourist attraction; one has only to look at the nearby Alston branch to see what *might* have been achieved between Rothbury and – perhaps – Brinkburn or Ewesley.

The Railway Today

The lines from Morpeth to Scotsgap and Rothbury have been closed and dismantled for many years, but the course of these abandoned routes can still be followed by road or on foot. Happily, some of the intermediate stations have found a new life as private dwellings, and for this reason Angerton and Meldon have both survived more or less intact. At Scotsgap, the site of the former goods yard has been redeveloped, while the station building is another private house; the old platform can still be discerned.

The Northumberland Central section is still substantially intact, and motorists on the nearby B6342 road can see much of the route as they head north towards Rothbury. Many stone-built overbridges survive along the lonely, grass-covered track that was once a railway, although Rothbury station has been submerged beneath an industrial estate. The most surprising survival is, perhaps, the wooden station building at Longwitton – this ramshackle structure has defied the demolition men for many years, and the old station (with its archaic wooden coach body) was still intact at the time of writing.

Addendum: Mines and Quarries

Enthusiasts and local historians hoping to trace the route of the branch will still find much of interest, not only in terms of railway infrastructure but also in connection with the various mines and quarries that once relied upon the railway for their transport needs. Unfortunately, many of these long-abandoned industrial ventures have disappeared more or less without trace, and it is particularly difficult to discover physical remains of the smaller mines and quarries. The history of local mining is also rather complicated in that different mining companies often tapped the same seams – producing inevitable confusion in the minds of modern researchers. With these cautionary thoughts in mind it is proposed to say a little more about some of the mines and quarries served by the railway, the first sites to be dealt with being those near Longwitton station.

In its 19th century heyday the Longwitton Colliery was a surprisingly large venture employing around 70 miners. It was situated about 1½ miles to the east of Longwitton station and 1 mile west of Longwitton village. The mine was linked to Longwitton goods yard by means of a tramway, traces of which can still be found. There was no mention of Longwitton Colliery in the officially-published *List of Mines worked under the Coal Mines Regulation Act* for 1900, suggesting that the pit had been closed in the 19th century. Much later, however, there is mentioned of a small drift mine known as Greenleighton Drift, and this presumably tapped the seams that had earlier been worked at Longwitton; this small-scale venture employed one miner and one surface worker, and as mentioned in Chapter Three, it was closed in November 1941.

There was, in addition to the coal mine at Longwitton, a quarry on the western side of the railway and this, too, was once linked to the main line by means of a siding connection. This quarry, worked by the Green Leighton Lime Company, was in operation in the 1870s, but it had apparently been abandoned by the turn-of-the-century.

The mineral lines at Fontburn were mentioned in Chapter Four, but it may be worth adding a few further details in this section. Whitehouse Quarry was listed in the *List of Quarries Working under the Quarries Act* for 1897 as a limestone quarry employing eight men; its owners were Armstrong & Co of 3, Bell's Terrace, North Shields and the location was given as 'near Ewesley station, N.Brit. Railway'. Subsequent editions of the *List of Quarries* show several minor changes. In 1898, for example, the quarry's labour force had risen to eleven men, while by 1899 the address of Armstrong & Co. had been changed to 'Whitehouse Quarries, via Morpeth'. The neighbouring Whitehouse Colliery was also worked by Armstrong & Co., and in 1900 they employed six miners and one surface worker at this small pit; the colliery does not appear in the 1910 *List of Mines* – suggesting that it had been exhausted by that date. Whitehouse quarry, meanwhile, had remained in operation; in 1922 it was worked by the Ewesley Quarry Co, and gave employment to nine men.

Moving northwards to Brinkburn, we find another cluster of mines and quarries within a very small area to the east of the railway. These appear to have been worked at a later date than the mines around Longwitton, though precise dating is made more problematic by the way in which certain pits were worked for a few years, then abandoned – and then re-opened (sometimes under a different name!). In the 1925 *List of Mines*, for example, the Lee Colliery was said to have been 'abandoned'. Its manager, George Dixon was, however, listed as the owner of nearby Chirm Colliery, and there was clearly a working relationship between these two mines.

Chirm Pit seems to have been worked successfully for many years; in 1899 it was owned by Jasper Fail of Longhorsley, and gave employment to 13 miners and 1 surface worker. In 1910 it was said to be producing household coal, and its combined underground and surface labour force was 14 men. The workforce had dropped to just eight by 1925, and as only two of these men were miners it is likely that the pit was nearing the end of its productive life by that time. The 1930 records make no mention of Chirm Pit but significantly 'R. Wood' (of 6, Kings Avenue, Morpeth) had opened a new mine at Healeycote, near Paperhaugh. This evidence suggests that local mining firms were following the local coal seams northwards, the oldest pits being around Longwitton while the later mining ventures were much nearer Rothbury.

As far as the Rothbury branch is concerned, it is important to remember the essentially temporary nature of mining and quarrying. It is, in particular, necessary to stress that the various mines and quarries *en route* from Scotsgap to Rothbury were not all worked at the same time – if they had been contemporary ventures, the line would have been much busier than it actually was! As a general rule, it could be said that Longwitton Colliery was worked in the 19th century, while Lee Colliery, Chirm Pit and Whitehouse mine were in operation during the later 19th and early 20th centuries. Thereafter, the emphasis shifted northwards to Healeycote Colliery (though some of the older pits were apparently re-entered by local miners who were able to extract coal that had been left by the larger operators).

The pattern of quarrying in and around Rothbury was less clear cut in that Ewesley Quarry, near Fontburn, remained in operation for many years, becoming more productive in the mid-20th century than it had been in earlier years (it was latterly producing around 500,000 tons of whinstone per annum). Other, much smaller quarries, were worked by local authorities and private builders to provide roadstone and building material, but these had less effect on the railway than the larger mining or quarrying ventures.

For convenience, a brief list of some of the more important mines and quarries served (directly or indirectly) by the Rothbury branch is given below. The list is by no means complete, but it will clarify the details mentioned above and in the previous chapters.

Table 3

MINES AND QUARRIES IN THE ROTHBURY AREA

Name	Product	Typical Workforce	Approximate Dates
Longwitton Colliery	coal	—	19th century
Green Leighton Quarry	limestone	—	19th century
Whitehouse Quarry	whinstone	41 (1922)	19th & 20th centuries
Whitehouse Colliery	coal	7 (1899)	Pre-1910
Lee Colliery (Brinkburn)	coal	n/a	Pre-1925
Chirm Colliery (Brinkburn)	coal	14 (1910)	1890–1928 (?)
Healeycote Colliery	coal	47 (1930)	c.1930–1940
Raw Colliery (Brinkburn)	coal	n/a	Pre-1910
Newhouses Quarry (Brinkburn)	stone	1 (1898)	1880s onwards
Wards Hill Quarry (Brinkburn)	limestone	2 (1922)	1880s onwards
Green Leighton Drift Mine	coal	2 (1941)	Closed 1941

Ex-NER class 'J21' 0–6–0 No. 65110 pounds through Longwitton with a down excursion in the 1950s. The long siding in the foreground once gave access to Longwitton Colliery; it was latterly used as a general siding. *E.E. Smith*

Appendix One
Chronological Table of Important Dates

1859	Wansbeck Railway empowered to build line from Morpeth to Reedsmouth.
1862	Wansbeck Railway opened to Scotsgap (July).
	Northumberland Central promoters meet at Morpeth (25th October).
	NCR plans lodged with local authorities (28th November).
1863	Further promotional meeting held at Morpeth (February).
	Wansbeck Railway absorbed by North British company (July).
	Northumberland Central Act receives Royal Assent (28th July).
1864	Proposed South Northumberland scheme for line southwards from Scotsgap.
	Wansbeck Railway opened to Knowesgate (7th June).
1865	Wansbeck Railway opened throughout to Reedsmouth (1st May).
1865	NCR Directors announce that they would proceed with construction of the southern part of their route (August).
1866	Economic crisis following failure of Overend, Gurney & Co (May).
	Richard Hodgson resigns as Chairman of the NBR.
1867	NCR obtains Act for abandonment of part of the 1863 route (12th April).
1869	NCR Directors resume construction with new contractors and Engineer.
	North British rejects proposed working agreement with NCR.
1870	New share and debentures issued to pay for construction of NCR.
	NCR line opened from Scotsgap to Rothbury (1st November).
1872	NCR absorbed by North British Railway (July).
	Rothbury branch train involved in breakaway incident (15th September).
1875	Branch train derailed in accident near Scotsgap (5th July).
1876	New facilities installed at Longwitton (February).
1877	North Eastern express crashes at Morpeth (18th March).
1884	Whitehouse limeworks siding installed at Fontburn (November).
1894	Refuge siding provided at Ewesley (August).
1899	Improvements at Rothbury station (October).
1902	Additional siding installed at Fontburn for reservoir traffic.
1903/4	Fontburn Halt opened as a public stopping place.
1923	North British Railway becomes part of LNER group.
1925	Brinkburn Coal Co. closes Lee Colliery.
1939	Outbreak of World War II; branch train service cut to 2 trains each way.
1947	Railways disrupted by severe Winter weather.
1948	LNER becomes part of British Railways (1st January).
1952	Rothbury branch passenger service withdrawn (13th September).
1963	Branch closed to all traffic (November).
1966	Wansbeck Railway closed to all traffic.

A detailed view of the distinctive down 'starters' at Scotsgap, on their raised lattice mast assembly (*see page 62 for other view*). *Barry Nicholson*

Appendix Two
Facilities at Rothbury and the Intermediate Stations

Rothbury

Passenger platform
Booking office and waiting room
Goods shed
Goods arrival line
Run-round loop
7 dead-end sidings for goods traffic and
    storage
Locomotive shed and turntable
Signal cabin
2-ton yard crane
Cattle pens
Weigh-house
Water tower
Old coach body (store), permanent way
    depot and stores

Brinkburn

Passenger platform
Booking office/waiting room
Station master's dwelling house
Goods siding
Goods lock-up
Lamp hut
Lever cabin (see notes)
Loading dock

Fontburn

Passenger platform
Waiting shelter
Railway cottages (2)
3 dead-end goods sidings
Tramway connections to Whitehouse
    Colliery, Whitehouse Limeworks &
    Ewesley Quarry
Lever cabin (see notes)

Ewesley

Passenger platform
Booking office/waiting room
Station master's dwelling house
Goods siding
Loading dock
Goods lock-up
Signal cabin
Refuge siding

Longwitton

Passenger platform
Booking office/waiting room
Goods siding (1 dead-end siding with
    'kick-back' spur)
Old coach body (store)
Loading dock
PW hut
Tramway connections to Longwitton
    Colliery and Limestone Quarry
Lever cabin (see notes)

Scotsgap Junction

Passenger platform
Booking office/waiting room
Goods sidings
Locomotive spur and turntable
Water tower and coaling stage
2-ton fixed yard crane
Loading docks/cattle pens
Weigh-house
Goods warehouse
Signal cabin
PW huts, stores, lamp room, etc

Notes

The facilities shown reflect the position c.1895–1905, when the Rothbury branch was at its peak in terms of industrial sidings, signalling and other infrastructure. There are one or two anomalies; at Longwitton, for instance, the goods siding is shown in addition to the two private sidings, whereas, in reality, the Longwitton Colliery siding seems to have been converted into an ordinary goods siding after the closure of the coal mine. It is also worth pointing out that the 'lever cabins' at Brinkburn, Fontburn and Longwitton were small single-storey signal boxes working both points and signals. A similar structure was provided at Ewesley, but as Ewesley was a crossing station its lever cabin had greater significance in terms of operation (Ewesley was, at one time, a block post). Rothbury and Scotsgap boxes were of course 'full' signal boxes in every sense of the term, and there is no doubt as regards their status.

Further Reading

There are few books or articles relating to the NBR lines in England, though happily there are signs that enthuasiasts are now appreciating the many attractions of these 'Scottish lines in Northumberland'. It is hoped that the following list of secondary works will be of use to those seeking further information on the Rothbury branch and connecting North British lines; for completeness, a few articles on suitable locomotives, etc., have been appended to the main list. (Articles marked * contain plans of interest to modellers).

R. Lendrom-Ainslie, Rothbury and the Wansbeck & Northumberland Central Sections of the NBR, *Railway Magazine*, January 1917 pp. 11–15.
C.R. Warn, *Rural Branch Lines of Northumberland* (1975).
Ian Futers, The Border Counties Railway, *Railway Modeller*, September 1976.*
       Northumberland Central, *loc.cit.*, November 1977, pp. 338–341.*
       Long Witton, *loc.cit.*, December 1977.
       Scotsgap Junction, *loc.cit.*, April, May, July 1983.*
       Wansbeck Valley, *Model Railways*, June 1978 pp. 296–303.*
C. Hamilton Ellis, A Border Branch, *Railway Magazine*, December 1985.
Robin McHugh, Two North British Locomotives, *Railway Modeller*, April 1983.
Don Rowland, An LNER Class J37, *Model Railways*, March 1972.
Richard Head, NBR as a Prototype for Modellers, *Railway Modeller*, July 1981.
John Thomas, *The North British Railway* (Vol. 1 1969, Vol. 2 1975).
C. Hamilton Ellis, *The North British Railway*
F. Coulton, Building a North Eastern G5, *Railway Modeller*, February 1967.
Nick Campling, Ex-NER Class A (F8), *Railway Modeller*, September 1972.*

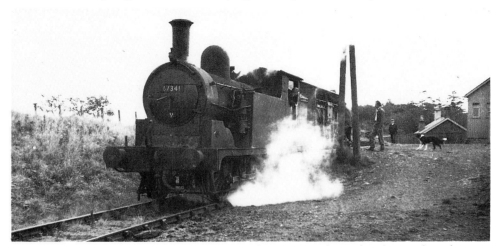

Class 'G5', 0–4–4T No. 67341 propels a cattle wagon into the single-siding goods yard at Ewesley. The date is 13th September, 1952. The station master's house is visible to the right.   *J.W. Armstrong*

Index